Knitting
for a
Cure

LEISURE ARTS, INC.
Little Rock, Arkansas

MW00352731

EDITORIAL STAFF

Vice President and Editor-in-Chief: Susan White Sullivan

Knit and Crochet Publications Director: Lindsay White Glenn

Special Projects Director: Susan Frantz Wiles

Director of E-Commerce: Mark Hawkins

Art Publications Director: Rhonda Shelby

Technical Writer: Linda A. Daley

Technical Editors: Sarah J. Green, Cathy Hardy, and Lois J. Long

Editorial Writer: Susan McManus Johnson

Art Category Manager: Lora Puls

Graphic Artist: Becca Snider

Imaging Technician: Stephanie Johnson

Prepress Technician: Janie Marie Wright

Photography Manager: Katherine Laughlin

Contributing Photographers: Jason Masters and Ken West

Contributing Photo Stylists: Angela Alexander
 and Sondra Daniel

Publishing Systems Administrator: Becky Riddle

Manager of E-Commerce: Robert Young

BUSINESS STAFF

President and Chief Executive Officer: Rick Barton

Vice President of Sales: Mike Behar

Vice President, Operations: Jim Dittrich

Vice President of Purchasing: Fred F. Pruss

Vice President of Finance: Laticia Mull Dittrich

Director of Corporate Planning: Anne Martin

National Sales Director: Martha Adams

Creative Services: Chaska Lucas

Information Technology Director: Hermine Linz

Controller: Francis Caple

Retail Customer Service Manager: Stan Raynor

Items made and instructions tested by Dale Potter.

Library of Congress Control Number: 2011943661

ISBN-13: 978-1-60900-420-0

TABLE OF CONTENTS

RACE FOR THE CURE

THE STREETS WERE A SEA OF PINK AND WHITE on October 22, 2011 in Little Rock, Arkansas. I watched the crowd, amazed at the thousands of pink ribbons worn by Race for the Cure entrants and onlookers. It was a wonderful sight, but of all the events related to the race that day, the one I'll always remember was the Survivors Parade.

Dozens of women in bright pink Survivor shirts walked behind a slow-moving float. On the float were the survivors whose illness or treatment made them too tired to walk that day—but they were there! They were smiling and excited about life. As we onlookers cheered for these women, I was moved to tears. These brave women were every color, size, and age. They were mothers, grandmothers, daughters, sisters, and wives. They gave us hope! And I could tell that the love and encouragement coming from the crowd—friends, family, and more than 40,000 strangers—gave the survivors hope, too.

These women are proof that if we continue to get the word out, we can make a difference in the fight against breast cancer. If you visit Komen.org, you will learn what everyone needs to know: Breast cancer strikes women and occasionally men from all backgrounds. Our best weapon against it is knowledge. We all need to perform self-exams, stay current on mammograms, and be aware of our family breast cancer history. Whenever we can, we should contribute to the search for a cure. Someday, I hope we will all be considered survivors because we'll have found the cure for breast cancer!

—Kay Meadors

MEET KAY MEADORS

HER MANY SKILLS INCLUDE SPINNING, WEAVING, AND QUILTING, but Kay Meadors is also a longtime designer of Leisure Arts knit and crochet books. Early in her career, Kay worked with us as an instruction writer. She later worked at home as a designer and pattern tester while home-schooling her son.

At Leisure Arts, we are always thrilled to open Kay's boxes of new designs, because truly wonderful afghans, christening sets, children's hats—the list is endless—have come from her clever hands. This latest pattern collection, Knitting for a Cure, is especially meaningful.

Kay says, "The journey of this book began a long time ago, when Denise Bell and I came up with the Traveling Shawl, a single project created by 50 different knitters. That one shawl covered our nation, passing from one caring knitter to another through each of the 50 states. Its pattern and the story of its journey are right here in this book that I am so pleased to share with you, because this is one of my favorite kinds of knitting—knitting with the heart.

"There are 18 knitted items to make as gifts, including a second, beaded version of the Traveling Shawl. As you can tell, my passion for shawls and lace knitting shines through. It is my hope that creating these projects will help you convey your love, thoughts, and prayers for someone who is fighting breast cancer."

Today, Kay loves to travel and teach knitting. Catch up with Kay at NaturalStateKnitter.blogspot.com, and find her books, including I Can't Believe I'm Lace Knitting, at LeisureArts.com. To learn more about the Traveling Shawl, visit Traveling50StatesShawl.blogspot.com.

The Journey of a Traveling Shawl

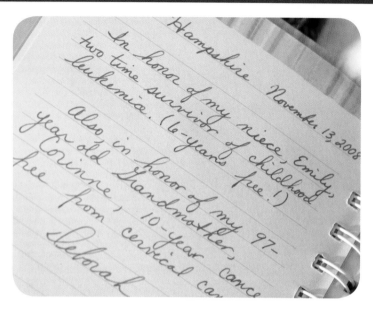

One hand-knit lace shawl of 32,548 stitches, created by 50 Ravelry™ knitters in 50 states in one year—I'm still amazed it really did happen.

I love my knitting to have purpose. I also love the camaraderie that exists around knitting and how people can knit while sharing their stories.

In 2008, I shared an idea with a friend I made through the online knit and crochet community, Ravelry.com. Denise Bell (LostCityKnits.com) and I were working on the same pattern. We compared progress and exchanged ideas, becoming friends even though we had never met in person.

My idea was to begin a shawl that would travel the 50 states. E-mails began to fly back and forth between us as Denise and I planned how to make this work. Denise said we needed a Ravelry group, and we both thought it would be great if the shawl could somehow benefit Susan G. Komen for the Cure.

In fact, what better cause could the Traveling Shawl support than breast cancer awareness and research?

Excited about this idea, Denise and I began planning. In just a few days, we had set up a blog, www.Traveling50StatesShawl.blogspot.com.

I visited every lace knitting group on Ravelry, peeked into their project folders to see examples of their lace knitting ability, and sent out many private messages. As word of the Traveling Shawl project began to spread, we had knitters asking to represent their states.

Along with the yarn, pattern, and needles, we mailed a journal so that each knitter could record what it meant for them to work on the shawl. State-by-state and row-by-row, the shawl grew. Most of the knitters wrote in the journal, telling stories of how they have been affected by cancer. Some shared their words on the blog.

In August 2009, the finished shawl returned to us. It had started out the year before as only a few skeins of yarn and a dream. It ran into a few speed bumps along the way—sickness and the everyday juggling of family, work, and life. There were times when we didn't know where the shawl was! Denise and I would worry and lose sleep, only to have the shawl get to the next state just fine. While the shawl was making its rounds from state to state, many thoughtful individuals who visited the blog made donations to Susan G. Komen for the Cure. In October 2009, we held a drawing to determine which of these donors would receive the shawl and the handwritten journal.

I now treasure the online blog journal, which tells the stories of the people in whose honor or memory the shawl was knitted. And I am so honored to know the 50 amazing knitters who made this happen. Several are breast cancer survivors, themselves.

If the story of the Traveling Shawl causes you to do anything, let it remind you to do a monthly self-examination and to stay current on your mammogram. Remind those you love to do so, too.

—Kay Meadors

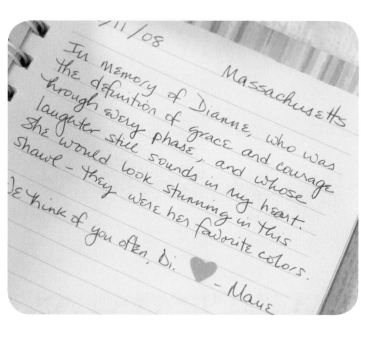

Fashion

When someone you know is fighting breast cancer, you want to offer all the encouragement you can. For the times you can't be there with them, it will help you both to know that your knitted gift is there. Your gift may offer warmth. It may offer luxury. Above all else, it will offer the comfort of your friendship and caring. And isn't that what knitting is all about?

TRAVELING SHAWL

The story of this heartwarming shawl, created by 50 knitters, is on page 4.

◖▬◻◻ **EASY +**

http://www.traveling50statesshawl.blogspot.com/
http://www.leisurearts.com/enews/archive/10_2009/YarnLink/InTheKnow.html

Finished Measurements:
Unblocked: 14" wide x 56¹/₂" long
(35.5 cm x 143.5 cm)
Blocked: 18" wide x 73¹/₂" long
(45.5 cm x 186.5 cm)

MATERIALS
Super Fine Weight Yarn
[1.76 ounces, 220 yards
(50 grams, 200 meters) per ball]:
   3 balls [approximately 630 yards (576 meters)]
Straight knitting needles, size 7 (4.5 mm) **or**
   size needed for gauge

GAUGE: In Stockinette Stitch,
         20 sts and 26 rows = 4" (10 cm)

Techniques used:
- YO **(Fig. 4a, page 89)**
- M1 **(Figs. 5a & b, page 90)**
- K2 tog **(Fig. 7, page 91)**
- SSK **(Figs. 9a-c, page 91)**
- Slip 1 as if to **knit**, K2 tog, PSSO
  (Figs. 12a & b, page 92)

When instructed to slip a stitch, always slip as if to **knit**.

FIRST EYELET EDGING
Cast on 81 sts **loosely**.

Row 1: Knit across.

Row 2 (Right side): Slip 1, K1, K2 tog, YO, K1, ★ YO, slip 1 as if to **knit**, K2 tog, PSSO, K2 tog, YO, K1; repeat from ★ across to last 4 sts, YO, SSK, K2: 69 sts.

Row 3: Slip 1, K1, purl across to last 2 sts, K2.

Row 4: Slip 1, K1, ★ K2 tog, YO, K1, YO, SSK; repeat from ★ across to last 2 sts, K2.

Row 5: Slip 1, K1, purl across to last 2 sts, K2.

Rows 6-29: Repeat Rows 4 and 5, 12 times.

BODY
Chart Readers: If desired, begin repeating Chart Rows 1-22, page 10, until Shawl measures approximately 52" (132 cm) from cast on edge, ending by working Row 16.

Row 1: Slip 1, K1, K2 tog, YO, K1, YO, SSK, ★ K5, K2 tog, YO, K1, YO, SSK; repeat from ★ across to last 2 sts, K2.

Row 2: Slip 1, K1, purl across to last 2 sts, K2.

Row 3: Slip 1, K1, K2 tog, YO, K2, YO, SSK, K3, K2 tog, ★ YO, K3, YO, SSK, K3, K2 tog; repeat from ★ across to last 6 sts, YO, K2, YO, SSK, K2.

Row 4: Slip 1, K1, purl across to last 2 sts, K2.

Row 5: Slip 1, K1, K2 tog, YO, K3, YO, SSK, K1, K2 tog, ★ YO, K5, YO, SSK, K1, K2 tog; repeat from ★ across to last 7 sts, YO, K3, YO, SSK, K2.

Row 6: Slip 1, K1, purl across to last 2 sts, K2.

Row 7: Slip 1, K1, K2 tog, YO, K4, YO, slip 1 as if to **knit**, K2 tog, PSSO, ★ YO, K7, YO, slip 1, K2 tog, PSSO; repeat from ★ across to last 8 sts, YO, K4, YO, SSK, K2.

Row 8: Slip 1, K1, purl across to last 2 sts, K2.

Row 9: Slip 1, K1, K2 tog, YO, K3, K2 tog, YO, K1, YO, SSK, ★ K5, K2 tog, YO, K1, YO, SSK; repeat from ★ across to last 7 sts, K3, YO, SSK, K2.

Row 10: Slip 1, K1, purl across to last 2 sts, K2.

Row 11: Slip 1, K1, K2 tog, YO, K2, K2 tog, YO, K3, YO, SSK, ★ K3, K2 tog, YO, K3, YO, SSK; repeat from ★ across to last 6 sts, K2, YO, SSK, K2.

Row 12: Slip 1, K1, purl across to last 2 sts, K2.

Row 13: Slip 1, K1, K2 tog, YO, K1, ★ K2 tog, YO, K5, YO, SSK, K1; repeat from ★ across to last 4 sts, YO, SSK, K2.

Row 14: Slip 1, K1, purl across to last 2 sts, K2.

Row 15: Slip 1, K1, (K2 tog, YO) twice, K7, ★ YO, slip 1 as if to **knit**, K2 tog, PSSO, YO, K7; repeat from ★ across to last 6 sts, (YO, SSK) twice, K2.

Row 16: Slip 1, K1, purl across to last 2 sts, K2.

Row 17: Slip 1, K1, ★ K2 tog, YO, K1, YO, SSK; repeat from ★ across to last 2 sts, K2.

Row 18: Slip 1, K1, purl across to last 2 sts, K2.

Rows 19-22: Repeat Rows 17 and 18 twice.

Repeat Rows 1-22 for pattern until Shawl measures approximately 52" (132 cm) from cast on edge, ending by working Row 16.

CHART

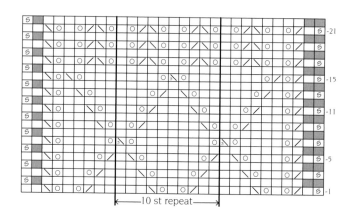

On RS rows, work Chart from **right** to **left**; on WS rows, work Chart from **left** to **right**.

KEY

- Ⓢ - Slip 1
- ☐ - K on RS; P on WS
- ■ - P on RS; K on WS
- ⊙ - YO
- ⊿ - K2 tog
- ◣ - SSK
- ◪ - slip 1, K2 tog, PSSO

SECOND EYELET EDGING

Row 1 (Right side)**:** Slip 1, K1, ★ K2 tog, YO, K1, YO, SSK; repeat from ★ across to last 2 sts, K2.

Row 2: Slip 1 , K1, purl across to last 2 sts, K2.

Rows 3-28: Repeat Rows 1 and 2, 13 times.

Row 29: Slip 1, K1, K2 tog, YO, K1, YO, SSK, ★ M1, K2 tog, YO, K1, YO, SSK; repeat from ★ across to last 2 sts, K2: 81 sts.

Row 30: Slip 1, knit across.

Bind off all sts **very loosely** in **knit**.

Care and Blocking Instructions: Gently hand wash Shawl and place on spin cycle in washer to remove excess water. Pin Shawl to desired blocked dimensions. Let dry completely. ♥

ENTRELAC SHAWL

This shawl is perfect to wrap around the shoulders of someone you love. See it in different shades of pink on page 19.

EASY +

Finished Measurements:

Unblocked: 46" across top x 26" across bottom x 11½" wide (117 cm x 66 cm x 29 cm)

Blocked: 66" across top x 36" across bottom x 16" wide (167.5 cm x 91.5 cm x 40.5 cm)

MATERIALS

Super Fine Weight Yarn

Version 1 (shown on page 19):
[1.75 ounces, 231 yards
(50 grams, 211 meters) per ball]:
   Lt Pink, Med Pink, **and** Dk Pink -
   One ball of **each** color

Version 2 (shown on page 13):
[1.76 ounces, 220 yards
(50 grams, 200 meters) per ball]:
   3 balls slow variegating
24" (61 cm) Circular knitting needle,
   size 7 (4.5 mm) **or** size needed for gauge
Crochet hook, size G (4 mm) for Edging

GAUGE: In Stockinette Stitch,
20 sts and 26 rows = 4" (10 cm)

Techniques used:

- YO *(Fig. 4a, page 89)*
- M1 *(Figs. 5a & b, page 90)*
- K2 tog *(Fig. 7, page 91)*
- P2 tog *(Fig. 8, page 91)*
- SSK *(Figs. 9a-c, page 91)*
- Slip 1 as if to **knit**, K2 tog, PSSO *(Figs. 12a & b, page 92)*
- Slip 2 tog as if to **knit**, K1, P2SSO *(Figs. 13a & b, page 93)*

STITCH GUIDE

KNIT INCREASE (uses one st)
Knit into the front **and** into the back of the next st.
PURL INCREASE (uses one st)
Purl into the front **and** into the back of the next st.

Do **not** cut yarn between Squares unless instructed. If you are using a slow variegating yarn as in Version 2, do **not** cut yarn at all.

FOUNDATION TIER

This Tier consists of 7 Triangles that make up the foundation of the Shawl.

FIRST TRIANGLE

With Dk Pink, cast on 2 sts.

Set-Up Row: Purl across.

Row 1 (Right side)**:** Knit increase, K1: 3 sts.

Row 2: Purl across.

Row 3: K1, M1, knit across: 4 sts.

Rows 4-25: Repeat Rows 2 and 3, 11 times: 15 sts.

Row 26: P 14, purl increase: 16 sts.

SECOND THRU SIXTH TRIANGLE

Row 1: With **right** side facing, cast on one st using backward loop method *(Fig. 2, page 89)*, knit increase, K1, leave remaining sts unworked: 3 sts on right needle tip.

Row 2 AND ALL WRONG SIDE ROWS THRU Row 24: Purl across.

Row 3: K1, M1, K2, leave remaining sts of previous Triangle unworked: 4 sts on right needle tip.

Row 5: K1, M1, K3, leave remaining sts of previous Triangle unworked: 5 sts on right needle tip.

Row 7: K1, M1, K4, leave remaining sts of previous Triangle unworked: 6 sts on right needle tip.

Row 9: K1, M1, K5, leave remaining sts of previous Triangle unworked: 7 sts on right needle tip.

Row 11: K1, M1, K6, leave remaining sts of previous Triangle unworked: 8 sts on right needle tip.

Row 13: K1, M1, K7, leave remaining sts of previous Triangle unworked: 9 sts on right needle tip.

Row 15: K1, M1, K8, leave remaining sts of previous Triangle unworked: 10 sts on right needle tip.

Row 17: K1, M1, K9, leave remaining sts of previous Triangle unworked: 11 sts on right needle tip.

Row 19: K1, M1, K 10, leave remaining sts of previous Triangle unworked: 12 sts on right needle tip.

Row 21: K1, M1, K 11, leave remaining sts of previous Triangle unworked: 13 sts on right needle tip.

Row 23: K1, M1, K 12, leave remaining sts of previous Triangle unworked: 14 sts on right needle tip.

Row 25: K1, M1, K 13, leave remaining sts of previous Triangle unworked: 15 sts on right needle tip.

Row 26: P 14, purl increase: 16 sts.

SEVENTH TRIANGLE

Rows 1-25: Work same as Second Triangle through Row 25: 15 sts on right needle tip.

Row 26: P 15: 105 sts.

Cut Dk Pink yarn.

TIER #1

This Tier consists of 8 Squares.

FIRST SQUARE

With **right** side facing and using Lt Pink, cast on 15 sts: 120 sts.

Set-Up Row: K 14, SSK (uses last st of cast on and one st of Last Triangle on Foundation Tier); leave remaining 14 sts of Triangle unworked: 15 sts on right needle tip.

Row 1: Slip 1 as if to **purl**, P 14.

Row 2 (Right side): K 14, SSK (uses last st on this Square and one st of Triangle on Foundation Tier); leave remaining sts of Triangle unworked.

Rows 3-27: Repeat Rows 1 and 2, 12 times; then repeat Row 1 once **more**.

Row 28: K 14, SSK (uses last st of Triangle on Foundation Tier).

SECOND THRU SEVENTH SQUARE
With **right** side facing, pick up 14 sts evenly spaced across end of rows of next Triangle on Foundation Tier *(Fig. 14a, page 93)*, K1 from **next** Triangle on Foundation Tier; leave remaining 14 sts of Triangle unworked: 15 sts.

Rows 1-28: Work same as First Square on Tier #1.

EIGHTH SQUARE
With **right** side facing, pick up 15 sts evenly spaced across end of rows of First Triangle on Foundation Tier: 15 sts.

Row 1: P 15.

Row 2 (Right side)**:** K 15.

Rows 3-28: Repeat Rows 1 and 2, 13 times: 120 sts.

Cut Lt Pink yarn.

TIER #2
This Tier consists of 9 Squares.

FIRST SQUARE
With **wrong** side facing and using Med Pink, cast on 15 sts: 135 sts.

Set-Up Row: P 14, P2 tog (uses last st of cast on and one st of last Square on previous Tier); leave remaining 14 sts of Square unworked: 15 sts on right needle tip.

Row 1 (Right side)**:** Slip 1 as if to **purl**, K 14.

Row 2: P 14, P2 tog (uses last st of this Square and one st of Square on previous Tier); leave remaining sts of Square unworked.

Rows 3-27: Repeat Rows 1 and 2, 12 times; then repeat Row 1 once **more**.

Row 28: P 14, P2 tog (uses last st of Square on previous Tier).

SECOND THRU EIGHTH SQUARE
With **wrong** side facing, pick up 15 sts evenly spaced across end of rows of next Square on previous Tier [these sts will be picked up **purlwise**, since they are picked up from the **back** side of the work *(Fig. 14c, page 93)*], slip last st picked up onto left needle tip and P2 tog with first st of **next** Square.

Rows 1-28: Work same as First Square on this Tier.

NINTH SQUARE
With **wrong** side facing, pick up 15 sts evenly spaced across end of rows of last Square on previous Tier (these sts will be picked up **purlwise**, since they are picked up from the **back** side of the work): 15 sts.

Row 1 (Right side)**:** K 15.

Row 2: P 15.

Rows 3-28: Repeat Rows 1 and 2, 13 times: 135 sts.

Cut Med Pink yarn.

TIER #3

This Tier consists of 10 Squares; the middle 8 Squares have a Lace Ribbon pattern.

FIRST SQUARE

With **right** side facing and using Dk Pink, cast on 15 sts: 150 sts.

Set-Up Row: K 14, SSK (uses last st of cast on and one st of last Square on previous Tier); leave remaining 14 sts of Square unworked: 15 sts on right needle tip.

Row 1: Slip 1 as if to **purl**, P 14.

Row 2: K 14, SSK (uses last st of this Square and one st of Square on previous Tier); leave remaining sts of Square unworked.

Rows 3-27: Repeat Rows 1 and 2, 12 times; then repeat Row 1 once **more**.

Row 28: K 14, SSK (uses last st of Square on previous Tier).

SECOND THRU NINTH SQUARE

With **right** side facing, pick up 14 sts evenly spaced across end of rows of next Square on previous Tier, K1 from **next** Square on previous Tier; leave remaining 14 sts of Square unworked: 15 sts.

Row 1: Slip 1 as if to **purl**, P 14.

Row 2: K 14, SSK (uses last st of this Square and one st of Square on previous Tier); leave remaining sts of Square unworked.

Rows 3-5: Repeat Rows 1 and 2 once, then repeat Row 1 once **more**.

Row 6: K4, YO, SSK, K3, K2 tog, YO, K3, SSK (uses last st of this Square and one st of Square on previous Tier); leave remaining 11 sts of Square unworked.

Row 7: Slip 1 as if to **purl**, P 14.

Row 8: K5, YO, SSK, K1, K2 tog, YO, K4, SSK (uses last st of this Square and one st of Square on previous Tier); leave remaining 10 sts of Square unworked.

Row 9: Slip 1 as if to **purl**, P 14.

Row 10: K6, YO, slip 1 as if to **knit**, K2 tog, PSSO, YO, K5, SSK (uses last st of this Square and one st of Square on previous Tier); leave remaining 9 sts of Square unworked.

Row 11: Slip 1 as if to **purl**, P 14.

Row 12: K6, K2 tog, YO, K6, SSK (uses last st of this Square and one st of Square on previous Tier); leave remaining 8 sts of Square unworked.

Row 13: Slip 1 as if to **purl**, P 14.

Row 14: K5, K2 tog, YO, K1, YO, SSK, K4, SSK (uses last st of this Square and one st of Square on previous Tier); leave remaining 7 sts of Square unworked.

Row 15: Slip 1 as if to **purl**, P 14.

Row 16: K4, K2 tog, YO, K3, YO, SSK, K3, SSK (uses last st of this Square and one st of Square on previous Tier); leave remaining sts of Square unworked.

Row 17: Slip 1 as if to **purl**, P 14.

Rows 18-21: Repeat Rows 16 and 17 twice.

Row 22: K6, YO, slip 2 tog as if to **knit**, K1, P2SSO, YO, K5, SSK (uses last st of this Square and one st of Square on previous Tier); leave remaining 3 sts of Square unworked.

Row 23: Slip 1 as if to **purl**, P 14.

Row 24: K 14, SSK (uses last st of this Square and one st of Square on previous Tier); leave remaining sts of Square unworked.

Rows 25-27: Repeat Rows 23 and 24 once, then repeat Row 23 once **more**.

Row 28: K 14, SSK (uses last st of Square on previous Tier).

TENTH SQUARE

With **right** side facing, pick up 15 sts evenly spaced across end of rows of last Square on previous Tier: 15 sts.

Row 1: P 15.

Row 2: K 15.

Rows 3-28: Repeat Rows 1 and 2, 13 times: 150 sts.

Cut Dk Pink yarn.

TIER #4

This Tier consists of 11 Squares.

FIRST SQUARE

Work same as First Square on Tier #2, page 15.

SECOND THRU TENTH SQUARE

Work same as Second Square on Tier #2.

ELEVENTH SQUARE

Work same as Ninth Square on Tier #2: 165 sts.

Cut Med Pink yarn.

TIER #5

This Tier consists of 12 Squares.

FIRST SQUARE

With **right** side facing and using Lt Pink, cast on 15 sts: 180 sts.

Set-Up Row: K 14, SSK (uses last st of cast on and one st of last Square on previous Tier); leave remaining 14 sts of Square unworked: 15 sts on right needle tip.

Row 1: Slip 1 as if to **purl**, P 14.

Row 2: K 14, SSK (uses last st of this Square and one st of Square on previous Tier); leave remaining sts of Square unworked.

Rows 3-27: Repeat Rows 1 and 2, 12 times; then repeat Row 1 once **more**.

Row 28: K 14, SSK (uses last st of Square on previous Tier).

SECOND THRU ELEVENTH SQUARE

With **right** side facing, pick up 14 sts evenly spaced across end of rows of next Square on previous Tier, K1 from **next** Square on previous Tier; leave remaining 14 sts of Square unworked: 15 sts.

Rows 1-28: Work same as First Square on Tier #5.

TWELFTH SQUARE

With **right** side facing, pick up 15 sts evenly spaced across end of rows of last Square on previous Tier: 15 sts.

Row 1: P 15.

Row 2: K 15.

Rows 3-28: Repeat Rows 1 and 2, 13 times: 180 sts.

Cut Lt Pink yarn.

TOP TIER

This Tier consists of 13 Triangles that make up the top edge of the Shawl.

FIRST TRIANGLE

With **wrong** side facing and using Dk Pink, cast on 15 sts: 195 sts.

Set-Up Row: P 14, P2 tog (uses last st of cast on and one st of last Square on previous Tier); leave remaining 14 sts of Square unworked: 15 sts on right needle tip.

Row 1: Slip 1 as if to **purl**, K 12, K2 tog.

Row 2: P 13, P2 tog (uses last st of this Triangle and one st of Square on previous Tier); leave remaining 13 sts of Square unworked: 14 sts on right needle tip.

Row 3: Slip 1 as if to **purl**, K 11, K2 tog.

Row 4: P 12, P2 tog (uses last st of this Triangle and one st of Square on previous Tier); leave remaining 12 sts of Square unworked: 13 sts on right needle tip.

Row 5: Slip 1 as if to **purl**, K 10, K2 tog.

Row 6: P 11, P2 tog (uses last st of this Triangle and one st of Square on previous Tier); leave remaining 11 sts of Square unworked: 12 sts on right needle tip.

Row 7: Slip 1 as if to **purl**, K9, K2 tog.

Row 8: P 10, P2 tog (uses last st of this Triangle and one st of Square on previous Tier); leave remaining 10 sts of Square unworked: 11 sts on right needle tip.

Row 9: Slip 1 as if to **purl**, K8, K2 tog.

Row 10: P9, P2 tog (uses last st of this Triangle and one st of Square on previous Tier); leave remaining 9 sts of Square unworked: 10 sts on right needle tip.

Row 11: Slip 1 as if to **purl**, K7, K2 tog.

Row 12: P8, P2 tog (uses last st of this Triangle and one st of Square on previous Tier); leave remaining 8 sts of Square unworked: 9 sts on right needle tip.

Row 13: Slip 1 as if to **purl**, K6, K2 tog.

Row 14: P7, P2 tog (uses last st of this Triangle and one st of Square on previous Tier); leave remaining 7 sts of Square unworked: 8 sts on right needle tip.

Row 15: Slip 1 as if to **purl**, K5, K2 tog.

Row 16: P6, P2 tog (uses last st of this Triangle and one st of Square on previous Tier); leave remaining 6 sts of Square unworked: 7 sts on right needle tip.

Row 17: Slip 1 as if to **purl**, K4, K2 tog.

Row 18: P5, P2 tog (uses last st of this Triangle and one st of Square on previous Tier); leave remaining 5 sts of Square unworked: 6 sts on right needle tip.

Row 19: Slip 1 as if to **purl**, K3, K2 tog.

Row 20: P4, P2 tog (uses last st of this Triangle and one st of Square on previous Tier); leave remaining 4 sts of Square unworked: 5 sts on right needle tip.

Row 21: Slip 1 as if to **purl**, K2, K2 tog.

Row 22: P3, P2 tog (uses last st of this Triangle and one st of Square on previous Tier); leave remaining 3 sts of Square unworked: 4 sts on right needle tip.

Row 23: Slip 1 as if to **purl**, K1, K2 tog.

Row 24: P2, P2 tog (uses last st of this Triangle and one st of Square on previous Tier); leave remaining 2 sts of Square unworked: 3 sts on right needle tip.

Row 25: Slip 1 as if to **purl**, K2 tog.

Row 26: P1, P2 tog (uses last st of this Triangle and one st of Square on previous Tier); leave remaining st of Square unworked: 2 sts on right needle tip.

Row 27: K2 tog.

Row 28: P2 tog (uses last st of Square on previous Tier).

SECOND THRU TWELFTH TRIANGLE

With **wrong** side facing, pick up 14 sts evenly spaced across end of rows of next Square on previous Tier (these sts will be picked up **purlwise**, since they are picked up from the **back** side of the work), slip last st picked up onto left needle tip and P2 tog with first st of **next** Square: 15 sts on right needle tip.

Rows 1-28: Work same as First Triangle on Top Tier.

LAST TRIANGLE

With **wrong** side facing, pick up 14 sts evenly spaced across end of rows of last Square on previous Tier (these sts will be picked up **purlwise**, since they are picked up from the **back** side of the work): 15 sts.

Row 1: Knit across to last 2 sts, K2 tog: 14 sts.

Row 2: Purl across.

Rows 3-26: Repeat Rows 1 and 2, 12 times: 2 sts.

Row 27: K2 tog; slip last st onto crochet hook for Edging.

EDGING

With crochet hook and working **very loosely** around entire Shawl, (slip st, ch 1) in every other row across end of rows and (slip st, ch 1) in each st across top/bottom of sts; join with slip st to first slip st, finish off.

Care and Blocking Instructions: Gently hand wash Shawl and place on spin cycle in washer to remove excess water. Pin Shawl to desired blocked dimensions. Let dry completely.

SLIP STITCH

To work a slip stitch, insert the hook in stitch or row indicated, yarn over and draw through stitch or row and through loop on hook *(Fig. A)* **(slip stitch made, abbreviated slip st)**.

Fig. A

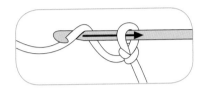

CHAIN

To work a chain, begin with a loop on the hook. Bring the yarn **over** the hook from back to front, catching the yarn with the hook and turning the hook slightly toward you to keep the yarn from slipping off. Draw the yarn through the loop *(Fig. B)* **(chain made, abbreviated ch)**.

Fig. B

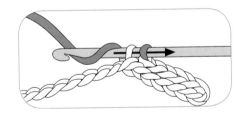

FINISH OFF

When you complete your last stitch, cut the yarn leaving a 4-6" (10-15 cm) end. Bring the loose end through the last loop on your hook and tighten it. ♥

HEADBAND & FINGERLESS GLOVES

For race day or every day, these cheery accessories are warm and encouraging.

EASY

HEADBAND

Finished Measurements:

Size Small - 18¹/₂" (47 cm) head circumference

Size Medium - 19³/₄" (50 cm) head circumference

Size Large - 21¹/₂" (54.5 cm) head circumference

Size Note: Materials are given for size Small, with sizes Medium and Large in braces { }. Follow the same instructions for all sizes. Finished measurements are obtained by using a different size needle as indicated in Materials.

MATERIALS

Medium Weight Yarn
[3.5 ounces, 218 yards
(100 grams, 199 meters) per hank]:
    One hank [approximately 100{110-120} yards/
    91.5{101-110} meters]
Straight knitting needles:
    Size Small - size 6 (4 mm)
    Size Medium - size 7 (4.5 mm)
    Size Large - size 8 (5 mm)
        OR SIZE NEEDED FOR GAUGE
Cable needle
Yarn needle
1¹/₄" (32 mm) Button
Sewing needle and matching thread

GAUGE: In Stockinette Stitch,
    Size Small - 22 sts and 28 rows = 4" (10 cm)
    Size Medium - 20 sts and 26 rows = 4" (10 cm)
    Size Large - 18 sts and 24 rows = 4" (10 cm)

Techniques used:
* M1 *(Figs. 5a & b, page 90)*
* K2 tog *(Fig. 7, page 91)*
* K3 tog *(Fig. 10, page 92)*

STITCH GUIDE

CROSS RIGHT *(abbreviated CR)* (uses 2 sts)
Knit into the **front** of the second st on the left needle, then **knit** the first st, letting both sts drop off the needle at the same time.

TWIST LEFT *(abbreviated TL)* (uses 2 sts)
Slip next st onto cable needle and hold in **front** of work, P1 from left needle, K1 from cable needle.

TWIST RIGHT *(abbreviated TR)* (uses 2 sts)
Knit into the **front** of the second st on the left needle, then **purl** the first st, letting both sts drop off the needle at the same time.

HEADBAND

Cast on 11 sts.

Row 1: K3, P2, K1, P2, K3.

Row 2 (Right side)**:** K5, P1, K5.

Row 3: K3, P2, M1, K1, M1, P2, K3: 13 sts.

Row 4: K3, CR, P3, CR, K3.

Row 5: K3, (P2, K3) twice.

Row 6: K5, P3, K5.

Row 7: K2, M1, K1, P2, M1, K3, M1, P2, K1, M1, K2: 17 sts.

Row 8: K4, CR, P5, CR, K4.

Row 9: K4, P2, K5, P2, K4.

Row 10: K6, P5, K6.

Row 11: K3, M1, K1, P2, M1, K5, M1, P2, K1, M1, K3: 21 sts.

Row 12: K5, CR, P7, CR, K5.

Row 13: K5, P2, K7, P2, K5.

Row 14: K7, P7, K7.

Row 15: K4, M1, K1, P2, M1, K7, M1, P2, K1, M1, K4: 25 sts.

Row 16: K6, CR, P9, CR, K6.

Row 17: K6, P2, K9, P2, K6.

Row 18: K8, P9, K8.

Row 19: K5, M1, K1, P2, M1, K9, M1, P2, K1, M1, K5: 29 sts.

Row 20: K7, CR, P 11, CR, K7.

Row 21: K7, P2, K 11, P2, K7.

Row 22: K9, P 11, K9.

Row 23: K6, M1, K1, P2, K 11, P2, K1, M1, K6: 31 sts.

Row 24: K8, CR, P 11, CR, K8.

Row 25: K8, P2, K 11, P2, K8.

Row 26: K 10, P 11, K 10.

Row 27: K8, P2, K 11, P2, K8.

Rows 28-52: Repeat Rows 24-27, 6 times; then repeat Row 24 once **more**.

Row 53: K8, P2, K2, P1, K8, P2, K8.

Row 54: K 10, P8, K1, P2, K 10.

Row 55: K8, P2, K2, P1, K8, P2, K8.

Row 56: K8, CR, P2, K1, P5, K1, P2, CR, K8.

Row 57: K8, P2, K2, P1, K5, P1, K2, P2, K8.

Row 58: K 10, P2, K1, P5, K1, P2, K 10.

Row 59: K8, P2, K2, P1, K5, P1, K2, P2, K8.

Row 60: K8, CR, P2, TL, P3, TR, P2, CR, K8.

Row 61: K8, P2, K3, (P1, K3) twice, P2, K8.

Row 62: K 10, P3, TL, P1, TR, P3, K 10.

Row 63: K8, P2, K4, P1, K1, P1, K4, P2, K8.

Row 64: K8, CR, P4, slip next 2 sts onto cable needle and hold in **back** of work, K1 from left needle, (P1, K1) from cable needle, P4, CR, K8.

Row 65: K8, P2, K4, P1, K1, P1, K4, P2, K8.

Row 66: K 10, P3, TR, P1, TL, P3, K 10.

Row 67: K8, P2, K3, (P1, K3) twice, P2, K8.

Row 68: K8, CR, P2, TR, P3, TL, P2, CR, K8.

Row 69: K8, P2, K2, P1, K5, P1, K2, P2, K8.

Row 70: K 10, P2, K1, P5, K1, P2, K 10.

Row 71: K8, P2, K2, P1, K5, P1, K2, P2, K8.

Row 72: K8, CR, P2, K1, P5, K1, P2, CR, K8.

Row 73: K8, P2, K2, P1, K5, P1, K2, P2, K8.

Row 74: K 10, P2, TL, P3, TR, P2, K 10.

Row 75: K8, P2, K3, M1, P1, K3 tog, P1, M1, K3, P2, K8.

Row 76: K8, CR, P4, slip next 2 sts onto cable needle and hold in **back** of work, P1 from left needle, P2 from cable needle, P4, CR, K8.

Row 111: K6, P2, K9, P2, K6.

Row 112: K6, CR, P9, CR, K6.

Row 113: K4, K2 tog, P2, K2 tog, K5, K2 tog, P2, K2 tog, K4: 21 sts.

Row 114: K7, P7, K7.

Row 115: K5, P2, K7, P2, K5.

Row 116: K5, CR, P7, CR, K5.

Row 117: (K3, K2 tog, P2, K2 tog) twice, K3: 17 sts.

Row 118: K6, P5, K6.

Row 119: K4, P2, K5, P2, K4.

Row 120: K4, CR, P5, CR, K4.

Row 121: K2, K2 tog, P2, K2 tog, K1, K2 tog, P2, K2 tog, K2: 13 sts.

Row 122: K5, P3, K5.

Row 123: K3, (P2, K3) twice.

Row 124: K3, CR, P3, CR, K3.

Row 125: K3, P2, K3 tog, P2, K3: 11 sts.

Row 126: K5, P1, K5.

Row 127 (button loop - first half)**:** K3, bind off next 5 sts, K2: 6 sts.

Row 128: K3, **turn**; add on 5 sts **tightly** (*Figs. 3a & b, page 89*) (button loop completed), **turn**; K3: 11 sts.

Row 129: Knit across.

Bind off all sts in **knit**, leaving a long end for sewing.

Thread yarn needle with long end. With **wrong** side together and matching rows, sew back seam.
Sew button to the end opposite the button loop.

Row 77: K8, P2, K 11, P2; K8.

Row 78: K 10, P 11, K 10.

Row 79: K8, P2, K 11, P2, K8.

Row 80: K8, CR, P 11, CR, K8.

Rows 81-104: Repeat Rows 77-80, 6 times.

Row 105: K6, K2 tog, P2, K 11, P2, K2 tog, K6: 29 sts.

Row 106: K9, P 11, K9.

Row 107: K7, P2, K 11, P2, K7.

Row 108: K7, CR, P 11, CR, K7.

Row 109: K5, K2 tog, P2, K2 tog, K7, K2 tog, P2, K2 tog, K5: 25 sts.

Row 110: K8, P9, K8.

FINGERLESS GLOVES

Finished Measurements:
   Size Small - 6" (15 cm) hand circumference
   Size Medium - 7¹/₃" (18.5 cm) hand circumference
   Size Large - 8" (20.5 cm) hand circumference

Size Note: Materials are given for size Small, with sizes Medium and Large in braces { }. Follow the same instructions for all sizes. Finished measurements are obtained by using a different size needle as indicated in Materials.

MATERIALS
   Medium Weight Yarn
   [3.5 ounces, 218 yards
   (100 grams, 199 meters) per hank]:
      One hank [approximately
      105{115-125} yards/96{105-114.5} meters]
   Set of 4 double-pointed knitting needles:
      Size Small - size 6 (4 mm)
      Size Medium - size 7 (4.5 mm)
      Size Large - size 8 (5 mm)
         OR SIZE NEEDED FOR GAUGE
   Cable needle
   Split-ring marker
   Scrap piece of yarn (to use as a st holder)
   Yarn needle

GAUGE: In Stockinette Stitch,
   Size Small - 22 sts and 28 rows = 4" (10 cm)
   Size Medium - 20 sts and 26 rows = 4" (10 cm)
   Size Large - 18 sts and 24 rows = 4" (10 cm)

Technique used:
• P2 tog *(Fig. 8, page 91)*

STITCH GUIDE

PURL INCREASE (uses one st)
Purl into the front **and** into the back of the next st.
KNIT INCREASE (uses one st)
Knit into the front **and** into the back of the next st.
CROSS RIGHT *(abbreviated CR)* (uses 2 sts)
Knit into the **front** of the second st on the left needle, then **knit** the first st, letting both sts drop off the needle at the same time.
TWIST LEFT *(abbreviated TL)* (uses 2 sts)
Slip next st onto cable needle and hold in **front** of work, P1 from left needle, K1 from cable needle.
TWIST RIGHT *(abbreviated TR)* (uses 2 sts)
Knit into the **front** of the second st on the left needle, then **purl** the first st, letting both sts drop off the needle at the same time.

LEFT GLOVE
WRIST

With double-pointed needles, cast 36 sts **loosely**.

Divide sts onto 3 needles *(see Double-Pointed Needles, page 88)*, placing 12 sts on each needle.

Place a split-ring marker around the first stitch to indicate the beginning of the round *(see Markers, page 87)*.

Rnds 1-3: ★ P1, K2, (P2, K2) twice, P1; repeat from ★ across each needle.

Rnd 4: ★ P1, CR, (P2, CR) twice, P1; repeat from ★ across each needle.

Rnds 5-20: Repeat Rnds 1-4, 4 times.

Rnd 21: (K 11, P1) across first needle, [P1, K2, (purl increase, P1) 3 times, K2, P1] across second needle, (P1, K 11) across third needle: 39 sts **total** (12 sts on first **and** third needles, 15 sts on second needle).

Rnds 22 and 23: (K 11, P1) across first needle, (P1, K2, P9, K2, P1) across second needle, (P1, K 11) across third needle.

Rnd 24: (K 11, P1) across first needle, (P1, CR, P6, K1, P2, CR, P1) across second needle, (P1, K 11) across third needle.

Rnd 25: (K 11, P1) across first needle, (P1, K2, P6, K1, P2, K2, P1) across second needle, (P1, K 11) across third needle.

GUSSET

Rnd 1: (K7, knit increase twice, K2, P1) across first needle, (P1, K2, P2, K1, P3, K1, P2, K2, P1) across second needle, (P1, K 11) across third needle: 41 sts **total** (14 sts on first needle, 15 sts on second needle, 12 sts on third needle).

Rnd 2: (K 13, P1) across first needle, (P1, K2, P2, K1, P3, K1, P2, K2, P1) across second needle, (P1, K 11) across third needle.

Rnd 3: [K7, (knit increase, K2) twice, P1] across first needle, (P1, CR, P2, K1, P3, K1, P2, CR, P1) across second needle, (P1, K 11) across third needle: 43 sts **total** (16 sts on first needle, 15 sts on second needle, 12 sts on third needle).

Rnd 4: (K 15, P1) across first needle, (P1, K2, P2, K1, P3, K1, P2, K2, P1) across second needle, (P1, K 11) across third needle.

Rnd 5: (K7, knit increase, K4, knit increase, K2, P1) across first needle, (P1, K2, P2, TL, P1, TR, P2, K2, P1) across second needle, (P1, K 11) across third needle: 45 sts **total** (18 sts on first needle, 15 sts on second needle, 12 sts on third needle).

Rnd 6: (K 17, P1) across first needle, (P1, K2, P3, K1, P1, K1, P3, K2, P1) across second needle, (P1, K 11) across third needle.

Rnd 7: (K7, knit increase, K6, knit increase, K2, P1) across first needle, [P1, CR, P3, slip next 2 sts onto cable needle and hold in **back** of work, K1 from left needle, (P1, K1) from cable needle, P3, CR, P1] across second needle, (P1, K 11) across third needle: 47 sts **total** (20 sts on first needle, 15 sts on second needle, 12 sts on third needle).

Rnd 8: (K 19, P1) across first needle, (P1, K2, P3, K1, P1, K1, P3, K2, P1) across second needle, (P1, K 11) across third needle.

Rnd 9: (K7, knit increase, K8, knit increase, K2, P1) across first needle, (P1, K2, P2, TR, P1, TL, P2, K2, P1) across second needle, (P1, K 11) across third needle: 49 sts **total** (22 sts on first needle, 15 sts on second needle, 12 sts on third needle).

Rnd 10: (K 21, P1) across first needle, (P1, K2, P2, K1, P3, K1, P2, K2, P1) across second needle, (P1, K 11) across third needle.

Rnd 11: (K7, knit increase, K 10, knit increase, K2, P1) across first needle, (P1, CR, P2, K1, P3, K1, P2, CR, P1) across second needle, (P1, K 11) across third needle: 51 sts **total** (24 sts on first needle, 15 sts on second needle, 12 sts on third needle).

Rnd 12: (K 23, P1) across first needle, (P1, K2, P2, K1, P3, K1, P2, K2, P1) across second needle, (P1, K 11) across third needle.

Rnd 13: (K7, knit increase, K 12, knit increase, K2, P1) across first needle, (P1, K2, P2, TL, P1, TR, P2, K2, P1) across second needle, (P1, K 11) across third needle: 53 sts **total** (26 sts on first needle, 15 sts on second needle, 12 sts on third needle).

Rnd 14: (K 25, P1) across first needle, [P1, K2, P3, slip next 2 sts onto cable needle and hold in **back** of work, P1 from left needle, P2 tog from cable needle, P3, K2, P1] across second needle, (P1, K 11) across third needle: 52 sts **total** (26 sts on first needle, 14 sts on second needle, 12 sts on third needle).

Rnd 15: (K7, knit increase, thread yarn needle with scrap piece of yarn, slip next 15 sts onto yarn for Thumb, K2, P1) across first needle, (P1, CR, P8, CR, P1) across second needle, (P1, K 11) across third needle: 38 sts **total** (12 sts on first needle, 14 sts on second needle, 12 sts on third needle).

HAND

Rnds 1 and 2: (K 11, P1) across first needle, (P1, K2, P8, K2, P1) across second needle, (P1, K 11) across third needle.

Rnd 3: [P1, K2, (P2, K2) twice, P1] across first needle, (P1, K2, P2 tog, P1, K2, P1, P2 tog, K2, P1) across second needle, [P1, K2, (P2, K2) twice, P1] across third needle: 36 sts **total** (12 sts **each** needle).

Rnd 4: ★ P1, CR, (P2, CR) twice, P1; repeat from ★ across each needle.

Rnds 5-7: ★ P1, K2, (P2, K2) twice, P1; repeat from ★ across each needle.

Rnd 8: ★ P1, CR, (P2, CR) twice, P1; repeat from ★ across each needle.

Bind off all sts **loosely** in pattern.

THUMB RIBBING

With **right** side facing, slip the first 7 sts from scrap yarn onto a double-pointed needle, slip last 8 sts onto a second double-pointed needle: 15 sts.

Rnd 1: With a third double-pointed needle, pick up one st at base of Hand (between sts on double-pointed needles) *(Figs. 14a & b, page 93)*, with same needle, K7, with an empty double-pointed needle, K8, place marker to indicate the beginning of the round: 16 sts (8 sts on **each** needle).

Rnd 2: Knit around.

Rnds 3 and 4: (P1, K2, P2, K2, P1) across each needle.

Bind off all sts **loosely** in pattern.

RIGHT GLOVE
WRIST

Work same as Left Glove through Rnd 23: 39 sts **total** (12 sts on first **and** third needles, 15 sts on second needle).

Rnd 24: (K 11, P1) across first needle, (P1, CR, P2, K1, P6, CR, P1) across second needle, (P1, K 11) across third needle.

Rnd 25: (K 11, P1) across first needle, (P1, K2, P2, K1, P6, K2, P1) across second needle, (P1, K 11) across third needle.

GUSSET

Rnd 1: (K 11, P1) across first needle, (P1, K2, P2, K1, P3, K1, P2, K2, P1) across second needle, (P1, K1, knit increase twice, K8) across third needle: 41 sts **total** (12 sts on first needle, 15 sts on second needle, 14 sts on third needle).

Rnd 2: (K 11, P1) across first needle, (P1, K2, P2, K1, P3, K1, P2, K2, P1) across second needle, (P1, K 13) across third needle.

Rnd 3: (K 11, P1) across first needle, (P1, CR, P2, K1, P3, K1, P2, CR, P1) across second needle, (P1, K1, knit increase, K2, knit increase, K8) across third needle: 43 sts **total** (12 sts on first needle, 15 sts on second needle, 16 sts on third needle).

Rnd 4: (K 11, P1) across first needle, (P1, K2, P2, K1, P3, K1, P2, K2, P1) across second needle, (P1, K 15) across third needle.

Rnd 5: (K 11, P1) across first needle, (P1, K2, P2, TL, P1, TR, P2, K2, P1) across second needle, (P1, K1, knit increase, K4, knit increase, K8) across third needle: 45 sts **total** (12 sts on first needle, 15 sts on second needle, 18 sts on third needle).

Rnd 6: (K 11, P1) across first needle, (P1, K2, P3, K1, P1, K1, P3, K2, P1) across second needle, (P1, K 17) across third needle.

Rnd 7: (K 11, P1) across first needle, **[**(P1, CR, P3, slip next 2 sts onto cable needle and hold in **back** of work, K1 from left needle, (P1, K1) from cable needle, P3, CR, P1)**]** across second needle, (P1, K1, knit increase, K6, knit increase, K8) across third needle: 47 sts **total** (12 sts on first needle, 15 sts on second needle, 20 sts on third needle).

Rnd 8: (K 11, P1) across first needle, (P1, K2, P3, K1, P1, K1, P3, K2, P1) across second needle, (P1, K 19) across third needle.

Rnd 9: (K 11, P1) across first needle, (P1, K2, P2, TR, P1, TL, P2, K2, P1) across second needle, (P1, K1, knit increase, K8, knit increase, K8) across third needle: 49 sts **total** (12 sts on first needle, 15 sts on second needle, 22 sts on third needle).

Rnd 10: (K 11, P1) across first needle, (P1, K2, P2, K1, P3, K1, P2, K2, P1) across second needle, (P1, K 21) across third needle.

Rnd 11: (K 11, P1) across first needle, (P1, CR, P2, K1, P3, K1, P2, CR, P1) across second needle, (P1, K1, knit increase, K 10, knit increase, K8) across third needle: 51 sts **total** (12 sts on first needle, 15 sts on second needle, 24 sts on third needle).

Rnd 12: (K 11, P1) across first needle, (P1, K2, P2, K1, P3, K1, P2, K2, P1) across second needle, (P1, K 23) across third needle.

Rnd 13: (K 11, P1) across first needle, (P1, K2, P2, TL, P1, TR, P2, K2, P1) across second needle, (P1, K1, knit increase, K 12, knit increase, K8) across third needle: 53 sts **total** (12 sts on first needle, 15 sts on second needle, 26 sts on third needle).

Rnd 14: (K 11, P1) across first needle, [(P1, K2, P3, slip next 2 sts onto cable needle and hold in **back** of work, P1 from left needle, P2 tog from cable needle, P3, K2, P1)] across second needle, (P1, K 25) across third needle: 52 sts **total** (12 sts on first needle, 14 sts on second needle, 26 sts on third needle).

Rnd 15: (K 11, P1) across first needle, (P1, CR, P8, CR, P1) across second needle, (P1, K1, knit increase, thread yarn needle with scrap piece of yarn, slip next 15 sts onto yarn for Thumb, K8) across third needle: 38 sts **total** (12 sts on first needle, 14 sts on second needle, 12 sts on third needle).

HAND

Rnds 1 and 2: (K 11, P1) across first needle, (P1, K2, P8, K2, P1) across second needle, (P1, K 11) across third needle.

Rnd 3: [P1, K2, (P2, K2) twice, P1] across first needle, (P1, K2, P2 tog, P1, K2, P1, P2 tog, K2, P1) across second needle, [P1, K2, (P2, K2) twice, P1] across third needle: 36 sts **total** (12 sts on each needle).

Rnd 4: ★ P1, CR, (P2, CR) twice, P1; repeat from ★ across each needle.

Rnds 5-7: ★ P1, K2, (P2, K2) twice, P1; repeat from ★ across each needle.

Rnd 8: ★ P1, CR, (P2, CR) twice, P1; repeat from ★ across each needle.

Bind off all sts **loosely** in pattern.

THUMB RIBBING
Work same as Left Glove. 🖤

CRESCENT SHAWL

Lightweight, lacy, and so lovely, this sweet wrap will be her favorite!

INTERMEDIATE

Finished Measurements:
Unblocked: 50" wide x 17" deep (127 cm x 43 cm)
Blocked: 68" wide x 22" deep (172.5 cm x 56 cm)

MATERIALS
Super Fine Weight Yarn **SUPER FINE 1**
[1.76 ounces, 220 yards
(50 grams, 200 meters) per ball]:
  3 balls [approximately 460 yards (421 meters)]
24" (61 cm) Circular knitting needle, size 8 (5 mm) **or** size needed for gauge

GAUGE: In Stockinette Stitch,
   18 sts and 24 rows = 4" (10 cm)

Techniques used:
- YO *(Fig. 4a, page 89)*
- K2 tog *(Fig. 7, page 91)*
- P2 tog *(Fig. 8, page 91)*
- SSK *(Figs. 9a-c, page 91)*
- P3 tog *(Fig. 11, page 92)*
- Slip 1 as if to **knit**, K2 tog, PSSO *(Figs. 12a & b, page 92)*
- Slip 2 tog as if to **knit**, K1, P2SSO *(Figs. 13a & b, page 93)*

Entire Shawl is knit in rows on a circular knitting needle. When instructed to slip a stitch, always slip as if to **knit**.

LACE EDGING
FIRST GARTER EDGE
Cast on 3 sts.

Knit 40 rows (20 garter ridges).

Bind off 2 sts, leaving last st on needle.

Working in end of rows, pick up one st in end of each garter ridge across *(Fig. 14a, page 93)*: 21 sts.

Foundation Row: K6, P 13, K2.

LACE

Chart Readers: If desired, begin repeating Chart Rows 1-22, 20 times.

Row 1 (Right side)**:** Slip 1, K1, K2 tog, YO, K 10, (K2 tog, YO) twice, K3.

Row 2: Slip 1, K2 tog, YO, K3, P 13, K2.

Row 3: Slip 1, (K2, YO) twice, SSK, K3, K2 tog, YO, K2, (K2 tog, YO) twice, K3: 22 sts.

Row 4: Slip 1, K2 tog, YO, K3, P 14, K2.

Row 5: Slip 1, K2, YO, K4, YO, SSK, K1, K2 tog, YO, K3, (K2 tog, YO) twice, K3: 23 sts.

Row 6: Slip 1, K2 tog, YO, K3, P 15, K2.

Row 7: Slip 1, K2, YO, K6, YO, slip 1 as if to **knit**, K2 tog, PSSO, YO, K4, (K2 tog, YO) twice, K3: 24 sts.

Row 8: Slip 1, K2 tog, YO, K3, P 16, K2.

Row 9: Slip 1, K2, YO, K7, K2 tog, YO, K5, (K2 tog, YO) twice, K3: 25 sts.

Row 10: Slip 1, K2 tog, YO, K3, P 17, K2.

Row 11: Slip 1, K2, YO, K7, K2 tog, YO, K1, YO, SSK, K3, (K2 tog, YO) twice, K3: 26 sts.

Row 12: Slip 1, K2 tog, YO, K3, P 18, K2.

Row 13: Slip 1, K1, K2 tog, YO, K2 tog, K4, K2 tog, YO, K3, YO, SSK, K2, (K2 tog, YO) twice, K3: 25 sts.

Row 14: Slip 1, K2 tog, YO, K3, P 17, K2.

Row 15: Slip 1, K1, K2 tog, YO, K2 tog, K3, K2 tog, YO, K3, YO, SSK, K2, (K2 tog, YO) twice, K3: 24 sts.

Row 16: Slip 1, K2 tog, YO, K3, P 16, K2.

Row 17: Slip 1, K1, K2 tog, YO, K2 tog, K2, K2 tog, YO, K3, YO, SSK, K2, (K2 tog, YO) twice, K3: 23 sts.

Row 18: Slip 1, K2 tog, YO, K3, P 15, K2.

Row 19: Slip 1, K1, K2 tog, YO, K2 tog, K3, YO, slip 2 tog as if to **knit**, K1, P2SSO, YO, K4, (K2 tog, YO) twice, K3: 22 sts.

Row 20: Slip 1, K2 tog, YO, K3, P 14, K2.

Row 21: Slip 1, K1, K2 tog, YO, K2 tog, K9, (K2 tog, YO) twice, K3: 21 sts.

Row 22: Slip 1, K2 tog, YO, K3, P 13, K2.

Rows 23-440: Repeat Rows 1-22, 19 times.

Do **not** cut yarn.

CHART

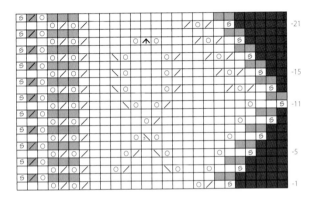

On RS rows, work Chart from **right** to **left**;
on WS rows, work Chart from **left** to **right**.

KEY
- ■ - No stich in area
- ⑤ - Slip 1
- □ - K on RS; P on WS
- ▨ - P on RS; K on WS
- ◉ - YO
- ╱ - K2 tog on RS
- ◪ - K2 tog on WS
- ╲ - SSK
- ◩ - slip 1, K2 tog, PSSO
- ⬆ - slip 2, K1, P2SSO

SECOND GARTER EDGE
Add on 3 sts (*Figs. 3a & b, page 89*): 24 sts.

Row 1 (Right side)**:** K2, K2 tog, leave remaining sts unworked.

Row 2: Turn; K3: 23 sts.

Rows 3-40: Repeat Rows 1 and 2, 19 times: 4 sts.

Row 41: K2, K2 tog: 3 sts.

Do **not** cut yarn.

BODY

With **right** side of Lace Edging facing, pick up 220 sts across the end of rows on Lace Edging (one st in each garter ridge), pick up 3 sts across the cast on edge of First Garter Edge: 226 sts.

Row 1: K3, purl across to last 3 sts, K3.

Row 2 (Right side)**:** Knit across.

Row 3: K3, purl across to last 3 sts, K3.

Row 4 (Decrease row)**:** K2, SSK, knit across to last 4 sts, K2 tog, K2: 224 sts.

Rows 5-13: Repeat Rows 3 and 4, 4 times; then repeat Row 3 once **more**: 216 sts.

Row 14: K2, SSK, (K3, K2 tog) across to last 2 sts, K2: 173 sts.

Row 15: K3, purl across to last 3 sts, K3.

Row 16 (Decrease row)**:** K2, SSK, knit across to last 4 sts, K2 tog, K2: 171 sts.

Rows 17-35: Repeat Rows 15 and 16, 9 times; then repeat Row 15 once **more**: 153 sts.

Row 36: K2, SSK, K1, (K2 tog, K2) across: 115 sts.

Rows 37-57: Repeat Rows 15 and 16, 10 times; then repeat Row 15 once **more**: 95 sts.

Row 58: K2, SSK, K2, (K2 tog, K1) across to last 8 sts, (K2 tog, K2) twice: 65 sts.

Rows 59-71: Repeat Rows 15 and 16, 6 times; then repeat Row 15 once **more**: 53 sts.

Row 72: K2, SSK, K1, K2 tog across to last 2 sts, K2: 29 sts.

Rows 73-79: Repeat Rows 15 and 16, 3 times; then repeat Row 15 once **more**: 23 sts.

Row 80: K2, SSK, K1, K2 tog across to last 2 sts, K2: 14 sts.

Row 81: K3, purl across to last 3 sts, K3.

Row 82: K2, K2 tog across to last 2 sts, K2: 9 sts.

Row 83: K2, P2 tog, P3 tog, K2: 6 sts.

Bind off remaining sts in **knit**.

Care and Blocking Instructions: Gently hand wash Shawl and place on spin cycle in washer to remove excess water. Pin Shawl to desired blocked dimensions. Let dry completely. ♥

BEADED TRAVELING SHAWL

This Shawl is a wisp of beaded elegance, sure to make the wearer feel special.

◼◼◻◻ EASY +

Finished Measurements:

Unblocked: 15¼" wide x 52¾" long
(38.5 cm x 134 cm)

Blocked: 20" wide x 62½" long
(51 cm x 159 cm)

MATERIALS

SUPER FINE
1

Super Fine Weight Yarn
[.88 ounce, 229 yards
(25 grams, 210 meters) per ball]:
2 balls [approximately 458 yards (419 meters)]
Straight knitting needles, size 8 (5 mm) **or**
size needed for gauge
84 (6-7 grams) Silver lined seed beads (size 6)
Fine crochet hook (optional)

GAUGE: In Stockinette Stitch,
18 sts and 24 rows = 4" (10 cm)

Techniques used:

- YO *(Fig. 4a, page 89)*
- M1 *(Figs. 5a & b, page 90)*
- K2 tog *(Fig. 7, page 91)*
- SSK *(Figs. 9a-c, page 91)*
- Slip 1 as if to **knit**, K2 tog, PSSO
  (Figs. 12a & b, page 92)

STITCH GUIDE

SLIP-BEAD-KNIT *(abbreviated SBK)* (uses one st)
Remove next st from left needle, slip a bead onto the st, then being careful not to twist the st, slip the st back onto the left needle and knit it.
A fine crochet hook may be helpful to pull st through bead.

When instructed to slip a stitch, always slip as if to **knit**.

FIRST EYELET EDGING

Cast on 81 sts **loosely**.

Row 1: Knit across.

Row 2 (Right side): Slip 1, K1, K2 tog, YO, K1, ★ YO, slip 1 as if to **knit**, K2 tog, PSSO, K2 tog, YO, K1; repeat from ★ across to last 4 sts, YO, SSK, K2: 69 sts.

Row 3: Slip 1, K1, purl across to last 2 sts, K2.

Row 4: Slip 1, K1, ★ K2 tog, YO, K1, YO, SSK; repeat from ★ across to last 2 sts, K2.

Row 5: Slip 1, K1, purl across to last 2 sts, K2.

Rows 6-29: Repeat Rows 4 and 5, 12 times.

BODY

Chart Readers: If desired, begin repeating Chart Rows 1-22, 11 times, page 40; then repeat Rows 1-16 once **more**.

Row 1: Slip 1, K1, K2 tog, YO, K1, YO, SSK, ★ K5, K2 tog, YO, K1, YO, SSK; repeat from ★ across to last 2 sts, K2.

Row 2: Slip 1, K1, purl across to last 2 sts, K2.

Row 3: Slip 1, K1, K2 tog, YO, K2, YO, SSK, K3, K2 tog, ★ YO, K3, YO, SSK, K3, K2 tog; repeat from ★ across to last 6 sts, YO, K2, YO, SSK, K2.

Row 4: Slip 1, K1, purl across to last 2 sts, K2.

Row 5: Slip 1, K1, K2 tog, YO, K3, YO, SSK, K1, K2 tog, ★ YO, K5, YO, SSK, K1, K2 tog; repeat from ★ across to last 7 sts, YO, K3, YO, SSK, K2.

Row 6: Slip 1, K1, purl across to last 2 sts, K2.

Row 7: Slip 1, K1, K2 tog, YO, SBK, ★ K3, YO, slip 1 as if to **knit**, K2 tog, PSSO, YO, K3, SBK; repeat from ★ across to last 4 sts, YO, SSK, K2.

Row 8: Slip 1, K1, purl across to last 2 sts, K2.

Row 9: Slip 1, K1, K2 tog, YO, K3, K2 tog, YO, K1, YO, SSK, ★ K5, K2 tog, YO, K1, YO, SSK; repeat from ★ across to last 7 sts, K3, YO, SSK, K2.

Row 10: Slip 1, K1, purl across to last 2 sts, K2.

Row 11: Slip 1, K1, K2 tog, YO, K2, K2 tog, YO, K3, YO, SSK, ★ K3, K2 tog, YO, K3, YO, SSK; repeat from ★ across to last 6 sts, K2, YO, SSK, K2.

Row 12: Slip 1, K1, purl across to last 2 sts, K2.

Row 13: Slip 1, K1, K2 tog, YO, K1, ★ K2 tog, YO, K5, YO, SSK, K1; repeat from ★ across to last 4 sts, YO, SSK, K2.

Row 14: Slip 1, K1, purl across to last 2 sts, K2.

Row 15: Slip 1, K1, (K2 tog, YO) twice, K7, ★ YO, slip 1 as if to **knit**, K2 tog, PSSO, YO, K7; repeat from ★ across to last 6 sts, (YO, SSK) twice, K2.

Row 16: Slip 1, K1, purl across to last 2 sts, K2.

Row 17: Slip 1, K1, ★ K2 tog, YO, K1, YO, SSK; repeat from ★ across to last 2 sts, K2.

Row 18: Slip 1, K1, purl across to last 2 sts, K2.

Rows 19-22: Repeat Rows 17 and 18 twice.

Rows 23-258: Repeat Rows 1-22, 10 times; then repeat Rows 1-16 once **more**.

CHART

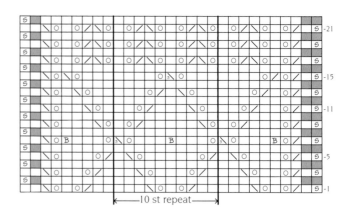

On RS rows, work Chart from **right** to **left**; on WS rows, work Chart from **left** to **right**.

KEY

⑤	- Slip 1
□	- K on RS; P on WS
■	- P on RS; K on WS
⊙	- YO
⧄	- K2 tog
⧅	- SSK
⧄	- slip 1, K2 tog, PSSO
Ⓑ	- slip-bead-knit (SBK)

SECOND EYELET EDGING

Row 1 (Right side)**:** Slip 1, K1, ★ K2 tog, YO, K1, YO, SSK; repeat from ★ across to last 2 sts, K2.

Row 2: Slip 1, K1, purl across to last 2 sts, K2.

Rows 3-28: Repeat Rows 1 and 2, 13 times.

Row 29: Slip 1, K1, K2 tog, YO, K1, YO, SSK, ★ M1, K2 tog, YO, K1, YO, SSK; repeat from ★ across to last 2 sts, K2: 81 sts.

Row 30: Slip 1, knit across.

Bind off all sts **very loosely** in **knit**.

Care and Blocking Instructions: Gently hand wash Shawl and place on spin cycle in washer to remove excess water. Pin Shawl to desired blocked dimensions. Let dry completely. ♥

TRAVELING SCARF

Patterned after the Traveling Shawl, this long scarf can be worn many ways!

■□□□ EASY +

Finished Measurements:
Unblocked: 5³/₄" wide x 67¹/₂" long
(14.5 cm x 171.5 cm)
Blocked: 7¹/₂" wide x 87³/₄" long
(19 cm x 223 cm) (blocked)

MATERIALS
SUPER FINE
1
Super Fine Weight Yarn
[1.76 ounces, 220 yards
(50 grams, 200 meters) per ball]:
2 balls [approximately 285 yards (261 meters)]
Straight knitting needles, size 7 (4.5 mm) **or**
size needed for gauge

GAUGE: In Stockinette Stitch,
20 sts and 26 rows = 4" (10 cm)

Techniques used:
- YO *(Fig. 4a, page 89)*
- M1 *(Figs. 5a & b, page 90)*
- K2 tog *(Fig. 7, page 91)*
- SSK *(Figs. 9a-c, page 91)*
- Slip 1 as if to **knit**, K2 tog, PSSO
  (Figs. 12a & b, page 92)

When instructed to slip a stitch, always slip as if to **knit**.

FIRST EYELET EDGING
Cast on 33 sts **loosely**.

Row 1: Knit across.

Row 2 (Right side): Slip 1, K1, K2 tog, YO, K1, ★ YO, slip 1 as if to **knit**, K2 tog, PSSO, K2 tog, YO, K1; repeat from ★ across to last 4 sts, YO, SSK, K2: 29 sts.

Row 3: Slip 1, K1, purl across to last 2 sts, K2.

Row 4: Slip 1, K1, ★ K2 tog, YO, K1, YO, SSK; repeat from ★ across to last 2 sts, K2.

Row 5: Slip 1, K1, purl across to last 2 sts, K2.

Rows 6-29: Repeat Rows 4 and 5, 12 times.

BODY
Chart Readers: If desired, begin repeating Chart Rows 1-22, page 44, until Scarf measures approximately 63" (160 cm) from cast on edge, ending by working Row 16.

Row 1: Slip 1, K1, K2 tog, YO, K1, YO, SSK, ★ K5, K2 tog, YO, K1, YO, SSK; repeat from ★ once **more**, K2.

Row 2: Slip 1, K1, purl across to last 2 sts, K2.

Row 3: Slip 1, K1, K2 tog, YO, K2, YO, SSK, K3, K2 tog, YO, K3, YO, SSK, K3, K2 tog, YO, K2, YO, SSK, K2.

Row 4: Slip 1, K1, purl across to last 2 sts, K2.

Row 5: Slip 1, K1, K2 tog, YO, K3, YO, SSK, K1, K2 tog, YO, K5, YO, SSK, K1, K2 tog, YO, K3, YO, SSK, K2.

Row 6: Slip 1, K1, purl across to last 2 sts, K2.

Row 7: Slip 1, K1, K2 tog, YO, K4, YO, slip 1 as if to **knit**, K2 tog, PSSO, YO, K7, YO, slip 1 as if to **knit**, K2 tog, PSSO, YO, K4, YO, SSK, K2.

Row 8: Slip 1, K1, purl across to last 2 sts, K2.

Row 9: Slip 1, K1, K2 tog, YO, K3, K2 tog, YO, K1, YO, SSK, K5, K2 tog, YO, K1, YO, SSK, K3, YO, SSK, K2.

Row 10: Slip 1, K1, purl across to last 2 sts, K2.

Row 11: Slip 1, K1, K2 tog, YO, K2, K2 tog, YO, K3, YO, SSK, K3, K2 tog, YO, K3, YO, SSK, K2, YO, SSK, K2.

Row 12: Slip 1, K1, purl across to last 2 sts, K2.

Row 13: Slip 1, K1, K2 tog, YO, K1, ★ K2 tog, YO, K5, YO, SSK, K1; repeat from ★ once **more**, YO, SSK, K2.

Row 14: Slip 1, K1, purl across to last 2 sts, K2.

Row 15: Slip 1, K1, (K2 tog, YO) twice, K7, YO, slip 1 as if to **knit**, K2 tog, PSSO, YO, K7, (YO, SSK) twice, K2.

Row 16: Slip 1, K1, purl across to last 2 sts, K2.

Row 17: Slip 1, K1, ★ K2 tog, YO, K1, YO, SSK; repeat from ★ across to last 2 sts, K2.

Row 18: Slip 1, K1, purl across to last 2 sts, K2.

Rows 19-22: Repeat Rows 17 and 18 twice.

Repeat Rows 1-22 for pattern until Scarf measures approximately 63" (160 cm) from cast on edge, ending by working Row 16.

SECOND EYELET EDGING

Row 1 (Right side): Slip 1, K1, ★ K2 tog, YO, K1, YO, SSK; repeat from ★ across to last 2 sts, K2.

Row 2: Slip 1, K1, purl across to last 2 sts, K2.

Rows 3-28: Repeat Rows 1 and 2, 13 times.

Row 29: Slip 1, K1, K2 tog, YO, K1, YO, SSK, ★ M1, K2 tog, YO, K1, YO, SSK; repeat from ★ across to last 2 sts, K2: 33 sts.

Row 30: Slip 1, knit across.

Bind off all sts **very loosely** in **knit**.

Care and Blocking Instructions: Gently hand wash Scarf and place on spin cycle in washer to remove excess water. Pin Scarf to desired blocked dimensions. Let dry completely. ♥

CHART

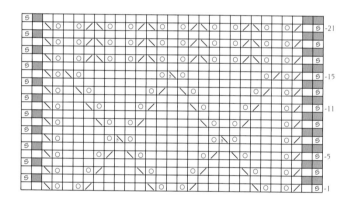

On RS rows, work Chart from **right** to **left**; on WS rows, work Chart from **left** to **right**.

KEY
⑤ - Slip 1
□ - K on RS; P on WS
■ - P on RS; K on WS
◎ - YO
╱ - K2 tog
╲ - SSK
◩ - slip 1, K2 tog, PSSO

STOCKING CAP

This Stocking Cap is a perfect match for the Scarf on page 50.

◖◻◻◻◻ **EASY**

Finished Measurements:

Size Small - 18¹⁄₂" (47 cm) head circumference
Size Medium - 19³⁄₄" (50 cm) head circumference
Size Large - 21" (53.5 cm) head circumference

Size Note: Instructions are written for size Small, with sizes Medium and Large in braces { }. Instructions will be easier to read, if you circle all the numbers pertaining to your size. If only one number is given, it applies to all sizes.

MATERIALS

Medium Weight Yarn **MEDIUM 4**
[3.5 ounces, 217 yards
(100 grams, 200 meters) per hank]:
   One hank
Straight knitting needles, size 8 (5 mm) **or**
   size needed for gauge
Cable needle
Yarn needle

GAUGE: In Stockinette Stitch,
            18 sts and 24 rows = 4" (10 cm)

Techniques used:

- M1 *(Figs. 5a & b, page 90)*
- K2 tog *(Fig. 7, page 91)*
- K3 tog *(Fig. 10, page 92)*

STITCH GUIDE

CROSS RIGHT *(abbreviated CR)* (uses 2 sts)
Knit into the **front** of the second st on the left needle, then **knit** the first st, letting both sts drop off the needle at the same time.

TWIST LEFT *(abbreviated TL)* (uses 2 sts)
Slip next st onto cable needle and hold in **front** of work, P1 from left needle, K1 from cable needle.

TWIST RIGHT *(abbreviated TR)* (uses 2 sts)
Knit into the **front** of the second st on the left needle, then **purl** the first st, letting both sts drop off the needle at the same time.

BAND

Cast on 19 sts.

Row 1: K2, P2, K 11, P2, K2.

Row 2 (Right side)**:** K4, P 11, K4.

Row 3: K2, P2, K 11, P2, K2.

Row 4: K2, CR, P 11, CR, K2.

Rows 5 thru 44{48-52}: Repeat Rows 1-4, 10{11-12} times.

RIBBON SECTION

Row 1: K2, P2, K2, P1, K8, P2, K2.

Row 2: K4, P8, K1, P2, K4.

Row 3: K2, P2, K2, P1, K5, P1, K2, P2, K2.

Row 4: K2, CR, P2, K1, P5, K1, P2, CR, K2.

Row 5: K2, P2, K2, P1, K5, P1, K2, P2, K2.

Row 6: K4, P2, K1, P5, K1, P2, K4.

Row 7: K2, P2, K2, P1, K5, P1, K2, P2, K2.

Row 8: K2, CR, P2, TL, P3, TR, P2, CR, K2.

Row 9: K2, P2, K3, (P1, K3) twice, P2, K2.

Row 10: K4, P3, TL, P1, TR, P3, K4.

Row 11: K2, P2, K4, P1, K1, P1, K4, P2, K2.

Row 12: K2, CR, P4, slip next 2 sts onto cable needle and hold in **back** of work, K1 from left needle, (P1, K1) from cable needle, P4, CR, K2.

Row 13: K2, P2, K4, P1, K1, P1, K4, P2, K2.

Row 14: K4, P3, TR, P1, TL, P3, K4.

Row 15: K2, P2, K3, (P1, K3) twice, P2, K2.

Row 16: K2, CR, P2, TR, P3, TL, P2, CR, K2.

Row 17: K2, P2, K2, P1, K5, P1, K2, P2, K2.

Row 18: K4, P2, K1, P5, K1, P2, K4.

Row 19: K2, P2, K2, P1, K5, P1, K2, P2, K2.

Row 20: K2, CR, P2, K1, P5, K1, P2, CR, K2.

Row 21: K2, P2, K2, P1, K5, P1, K2, P2, K2.

Row 22: K4, P2, TL, P3, TR, P2, K4.

Row 23: K2, P2, K3, M1, P1, K3 tog, P1, M1, K3, P2, K2.

Row 24: K2, CR, P4, slip next 2 sts onto cable needle and hold in **back** of work, P1 from left needle, P2 from cable needle, P4, CR, K2.

Row 25: K2, P2, K 11, P2, K2.

Row 26: K4, P 11, K4.

Row 27: K2, P2, K 11, P2, K2.

Row 28: K2, CR, P 11, CR, K2.

Rows 29 thru 67{71-75}: Repeat Rows 25-28, 9{10-11} times; then repeat Rows 25-27 once **more**.

Bind off all sts in pattern, leaving last st on needle for Top.

TOP

With **right** side facing, pick up 84{91-100} sts evenly spaced along edge of Band **(Fig. 14a, page 93)**: 85{92-101} sts.

Row 1: Purl across.

Row 2: Knit across.

Rows 3-5: Repeat Rows 1 and 2 once, then repeat Row 1 once **more**.

Row 6: Knit across decreasing 4{1-0} st(s) evenly spaced **(see Zeros, page 88)**: 81{91-101} sts.

Repeat Rows 1 and 2, 1{1-2} time(s); then repeat Row 1 once **more**.

SHAPING
Row 1: (K8, K2 tog) across to last st, K1: 73{82-91} sts.

Row 2 AND ALL WRONG SIDE ROWS: Purl across.

Row 3: (K7, K2 tog) across to last st, K1: 65{73-81} sts.

Row 5: (K6, K2 tog) across to last st, K1: 57{64-71} sts.

Row 7: (K5, K2 tog) across to last st, K1: 49{55-61} sts.

Row 9: (K4, K2 tog) across to last st, K1: 41{46-51} sts.

Row 11: (K3, K2 tog) across to last st, K1: 33{37-41} sts.

Row 13: (K2, K2 tog) across to last st, K1: 25{28-31} sts.

Row 15: (K1, K2 tog) across to last st, K1: 17{19-21} sts.

Row 17: K2 tog across to last st, K1: 9{10-11} sts.

Cut yarn, leaving a long end for sewing.

FINISHING
Thread yarn needle with yarn end and slip remaining 9{10-11} sts onto needle; pull **tightly** to gather and secure end but do **not** cut yarn.
With **right** side together, sew seam. 💜

SCARF

So pretty, so cozy! Pair with the Stocking Cap on page 46 for a toasty set.

■■□□ EASY

Finished Measurement:
4¹/₄" wide x 72" long (11 cm x 183 cm)

MATERIALS

Medium Weight Yarn
[3.5 ounces, 217 yards
(100 grams, 200 meters) per hank]:
   2 hanks
Straight knitting needles, size 8 (5 mm) **or**
   size needed for gauge
Cable needle
Yarn needle

GAUGE: In Stockinette Stitch,
18 sts and 24 rows = 4" (10 cm)

Techniques used:
- M1 *(Figs. 5a & b, page 90)*
- K3 tog *(Fig. 10, page 92)*

STITCH GUIDE

CROSS RIGHT *(abbreviated CR)* (uses 2 sts)
Knit into the **front** of the second st on the left needle, then **knit** the first st, letting both sts drop off the needle at the same time.
TWIST LEFT *(abbreviated TL)* (uses 2 sts)
Slip next st onto cable needle and hold in **front** of work, P1 from left needle, K1 from cable needle.
TWIST RIGHT *(abbreviated TR)* (uses 2 sts)
Knit into the **front** of the second st on the left needle, then **purl** the first st, letting both sts drop off the needle at the same time.

SCARF
FIRST HALF

Cast on 19 sts.

Row 1: K2, P2, K 11, P2, K2.

Row 2 (Right side)**:** Knit across.

Row 3: K2, P2, K 11, P2, K2.

Row 4: K2, CR, K 11, CR, K2.

Row 5: K2, P2, K 11, P2, K2.

Row 6: K4, P 11, K4.

Row 7: K2, P2, K 11, P2, K2.

Row 8: K2, CR, P 11, CR, K2.

Row 9: K2, P2, K2, P1, K8, P2, K2.

Row 10: K4, P8, K1, P2, K4.

Row 11: K2, P2, K2, P1, K5, P1, K2, P2, K2.

Row 12: K2, CR, P2, K1, P5, K1, P2, CR, K2.

Row 13: K2, P2, K2, P1, K5, P1, K2, P2, K2.

Row 14: K4, P2, K1, P5, K1, P2, K4.

Row 15: K2, P2, K2, P1, K5, P1, K2, P2, K2.

Row 16: K2, CR, P2, TL, P3, TR, P2, CR, K2.

Row 17: K2, P2, K3, (P1, K3) twice, P2, K2.

Row 18: K4, P3, TL, P1, TR, P3, K4.

Row 19: K2, P2, K4, P1, K1, P1, K4, P2, K2.

Row 20: K2, CR, P4, slip next 2 sts onto cable needle and hold in **back** of work, K1 from left needle, (P1, K1) from cable needle, P4, CR, K2.

Row 21: K2, P2, K4, P1, K1, P1, K4, P2, K2.

Row 22: K4, P3, TR, P1, TL, P3, K4.

Row 23: K2, P2, K3, (P1, K3) twice, P2, K2.

Row 24: K2, CR, P2, TR, P3, TL, P2, CR, K2.

Row 25: K2, P2, K2, P1, K5, P1, K2, P2, K2.

Row 26: K4, P2, K1, P5, K1, P2, K4.

Row 27: K2, P2, K2, P1, K5, P1, K2, P2, K2.

Row 28: K2, CR, P2, K1, P5, K1, P2, CR, K2.

Row 29: K2, P2, K2, P1, K5, P1, K2, P2, K2.

Row 30: K4, P2, TL, P3, TR, P2, K4.

Row 31: K2, P2, K3, M1, P1, K3 tog, P1, M1, K3, P2, K2.

Row 32: K2, CR, P4, slip next 2 sts onto cable needle and hold in **back** of work, P1 from left needle, P2 from cable needle, P4, CR, K2.

Row 33: K2, P2, K 11, P2, K2.

Row 34: K4, P 11, K4.

Row 35: K2, P2, K 11, P2, K2.

Row 36: K2, CR, P 11, CR, K2.

Row 37: K2, P2, K 11, P2, K2.

Row 38: Knit across.

Row 39: K2, P2, K 11, P2, K2.

Row 40: K2, CR, K 11, CR, K2.

Repeat Rows 37-40 for pattern until First Half measures approximately 36" (91.5 cm) from cast on edge, ending by working Row 38.

Bind off sts in pattern, leaving a long end for sewing.

SECOND HALF
Work same as First Half.

With **right** sides together and matching bound off sts, sew both pieces together. ♥

Home

Show your support with knitting! Why not cheer a survivor with a tea cozy? Or make her feel cozy with a hot water bottle cover? Pink-ribbon accessories can be as simple as a bookmark, or as enduring as a lap throw. Be sure to make a quick mug warmer for all your friends—you'll have fun while providing a gentle reminder!

FACE CLOTH

A soft Face Cloth, paired with a luxurious bar of soap
in a lovely matching soap cover on page 80—what a thoughtful gift!

◼◼◻◻ **INTERMEDIATE**

Finished Measurements:
 Unblocked: 12¹/₂" (32 cm) square
 Blocked: 13³/₄" (35 cm) square

MATERIALS

Light Weight Yarn 🧶 **3** LIGHT
[1³/₄ ounces, 110 yards
(50 grams, 100 meters) per skein]:
  One skein
Set of 5 double-pointed knitting needles,
  size 7 (4.5 mm) **or** size needed for gauge
16" (40.5 cm) Circular knitting needle,
  size 7 (4.5 mm)
Split-ring marker

GAUGE: In Stockinette Stitch,
    20 sts and 28 rnds = 4" (10 cm)

Techniques used:

* YO **(Fig. 4a, page 89)**
* K2 tog **(Fig. 7, page 91)**
* SSK **(Figs. 9a-c, page 91)**
* Slip 1 as if to **knit**, K2 tog, PSSO
  (Figs. 12a & b, page 92)
* Slip 2 tog as if to **knit**, K1, P2SSO
  (Figs. 13a & b, page 93)

FACE CLOTH

With double-pointed needles, cast on 8 sts.

Divide sts onto 4 needles **(see Double-Pointed Needles, page 88)**, placing 2 sts on each needle.

Place a split-ring marker around the first stitch to indicate the beginning of the round **(see Markers, page 87)**.

Rnd 1 AND ALL ODD NUMBERED RNDS: Knit around.

Rnd 2: (K1, YO) around: 16 sts total (4 sts **each** needle).

Rnd 4: ★ K1, YO, K3, YO; repeat from ★ around: 24 sts total (6 sts **each** needle).

Rnd 6: ★ K1, YO, K5, YO; repeat from ★ around: 32 sts total (8 sts **each** needle).

Rnd 8: ★ K1, YO, K7, YO; repeat from ★ around: 40 sts total (10 sts **each** needle).

Rnd 10: ★ K1, YO, K2, K2 tog, YO, K1, YO, SSK, K2, YO; repeat from ★ around: 48 sts total (12 sts **each** needle).

Rnd 12: ★ (K1, YO) twice, (SSK, K2 tog, YO, K1, YO) twice; repeat from ★ around: 56 sts total (14 sts **each** needle).

Rnd 14: ★ K1, YO, K 13, YO; repeat from ★ around: 64 sts total (16 sts **each** needle).

Rnd 16: ★ K1, YO, K 15, YO; repeat from ★ around: 72 sts total (18 sts **each** needle).

Rnd 18: ★ K1, YO, K5, YO, SSK, K3, K2 tog, YO, K5, YO; repeat from ★ around: 80 sts total (20 sts **each** needle).

Rnd 20: ★ K1, YO, K7, YO, SSK, K1, K2 tog, YO, K7, YO; repeat from ★ around: 88 sts total (22 sts **each** needle).

Rnd 22: With circular knitting needle, ★ K1, YO, K9, YO, slip 1 as if to **knit**, K2 tog, PSSO, YO, K9, YO; repeat from ★ around; place marker on right-hand needle to mark the beginning of the rnd: 96 sts.

Rnd 24: ★ K1, YO, K 10, K2 tog, YO, K 11, YO; repeat from ★ around: 104 sts.

Rnd 26: ★ K1, YO, K 10, K2 tog, YO, K1, YO, SSK, K 10, YO; repeat from ★ around: 112 sts.

Rnd 28: ★ K1, YO, K 10, K2 tog, YO, K3, YO, SSK, K 10, YO; repeat from ★ around: 120 sts.

Rnd 30: ★ K1, YO, K 11, K2 tog, YO, K3, YO, SSK, K 11, YO; repeat from ★ around: 128 sts.

Rnd 32: ★ K1, YO, K 12, K2 tog, YO, K3, YO, SSK, K 12, YO; repeat from ★ around: 136 sts.

Rnd 34: ★ K1, YO, K 15, YO, slip 2 tog as if to **knit**, K1, P2SSO, YO, K 15, YO; repeat from ★ around: 144 sts.

Rnd 36: ★ K1, YO, K 35, YO; repeat from ★ around: 152 sts.

Rnd 38: ★ K1, YO, K 37, YO; repeat from ★ around: 160 sts.

Rnd 40: ★ K1, YO, K2, (K2 tog, YO, K1, YO, SSK) 7 times, K2, YO; repeat from ★ around: 168 sts.

Rnd 42: ★ (K1, YO) twice, (SSK, K2 tog, YO, K1, YO) 8 times; repeat from ★ around: 176 sts.

Rnd 44: ★ K1, YO, K2, YO, SSK, (K2 tog, YO, K1, YO, SSK) 7 times, K2 tog, YO, K2, YO; repeat from ★ around: 184 sts.

Bind off all sts **very loosely** in **purl**.

Care and Blocking Instructions: Gently hand wash in no-rinse Wool wash. Place in a clean towel and gently press out excess water. Pin Face Cloth to desired blocked dimensions. Let dry completely. ♥

BOOKMARK

A bookmark is an easy project. For a comforting gift, pair it with a book of devotions or a daily journal.

EASY

Finished Measurement:

2" wide x 6¼" long (5 cm x 16 cm)

MATERIALS

100% Cotton Super Fine Weight Yarn **SUPER FINE 1**
[150 yards (137 meters) per ball]:
   One ball [approximately 20 yards (18.5 meters)]
Straight knitting needles, size 2 (2.75 mm) **or**
   size needed for gauge
Cable needle

GAUGE: In pattern,
15 sts and 18 rows = 2" (5 cm)

Techniques used:
- M1 **(Figs. 5a & b, page 90)**
- K3 tog **(Fig. 10, page 92)**

STITCH GUIDE

TWIST LEFT *(abbreviated TL)* (uses 2 sts)
Slip next st onto cable needle and hold in **front** of work, P1 from left needle, K1 from cable needle.
TWIST RIGHT *(abbreviated TR)* (uses 2 sts)
Knit into the **front** of the second st on the left needle, then **purl** the first st, letting both sts drop off the needle at the same time.

BOOKMARK

Cast on 15 sts.

Set-Up Row: Knit across.

Row 1 (Right side)**:** K2, P 11, K2.

Row 2: Knit across.

Row 3: K2, P 11, K2.

Row 4: K4, P1, K 10.

Row 5: K2, P8, K1, P2, K2.

Row 6: K4, P1, K 10.

Row 7: K2, P2, K1, P5, K1, P2, K2.

Row 8: K4, P1, K5, P1, K4.

Rows 9 and 10: Repeat Rows 7 and 8.

Row 11: K2, P2, TL, P3, TR, P2, K2.

Row 12: K5, P1, K3, P1, K5.

Row 13: K2, P3, TL, P1, TR, P3, K2.

Row 14: K6, P1, K1, P1, K6.

Row 15: K2, P4, slip next 2 sts onto cable needle and hold in **back** of work, K1 from left needle, (P1, K1) from cable needle, P4, K2.

Row 16: K6, P1, K1, P1, K6.

Row 17: K2, P3, TR, P1, TL, P3, K2.

Row 18: K5, P1, K3, P1, K5.

Row 19: K2, P2, TR, P3, TL, P2, K2.

Row 20: K4, P1, K5, P1, K4.

Row 21: K2, P2, K1, P5, K1, P2, K2.

Rows 22-24: Repeat Rows 20 and 21 once, then repeat Row 20 once **more**.

Row 25: K2, P2, TL, P3, TR, P2, K2.

Row 26: K5, M1, P1, K3 tog, P1, M1, K5.

Row 27: K2, P4, slip next 2 sts onto cable needle and hold in **back** of work, P1 from left needle, P2 from cable needle, P4, K2.

Rows 28-53: Repeat Rows 2-27.

Rows 54-56: Repeat Rows 2 and 3 once, then repeat Row 2 once **more**.

Bind off all sts in pattern. 💙

CARD INSERT

This Card Insert is a perfect and simple way to make a meaningful card. To give as a set of stationery, make several cards and use pink or white ribbon to bundle them together.

Finished Measurement:
4" wide x 5¹/₂" long (10 cm x 14 cm)

MATERIALS

100% Cotton Super Fine Weight Yarn
[150 yards (137 meters) per ball]:
 One ball [approximately 40 yards (36.5 meters)
 for **each** Insert]
Straight knitting needles, size 2 (2.75 mm) **or**
 size needed for gauge
Cable needle
Photo frame cards - 5" x 6⁷/₈" (12.5 cm x 17.5 cm)
 with a window opening of 3¹/₈" x 4⁵/₈"
 (8 cm x 11.5 cm)
 We used Strathmore Photo Frame Cards
 www.strathmoreartist.com
Spray starch
Glue

GAUGE: In Stockinette Stitch,
 14 sts and 18 rows = 2" (5 cm)

Techniques used:
- M1 *(Figs. 5a & b, page 90)*
- K3 tog *(Fig. 10, page 92)*

STITCH GUIDE

TWIST LEFT *(abbreviated TL)* (uses 2 sts)
Slip next st onto cable needle and hold in **front** of work, P1 from left needle, K1 from cable needle.
TWIST RIGHT *(abbreviated TR)* (uses 2 sts)
Knit into the **front** of the second st on the left needle, then **purl** the first st, letting both sts drop off the needle at the same time.

INSERT

Cast on 29 sts.

Row 1: Knit across.

Row 2 (Right side)**:** K2, purl across to last 2 sts, K2.

Rows 3-9: Repeat Rows 1 and 2, 3 times; then repeat Row 1 once **more**.

Row 10: K2, P 16, K1, P8, K2.

Row 11: K 10, P1, K 18.

Row 12: K2, P 16, K1, P8, K2.

Row 13: K 10, P1, K7, P1, K 10.

Row 14: K2, P8, K1, P7, K1, P8, K2.

Rows 15-17: Repeat Rows 13 and 14 once, then repeat Row 13 once **more**.

Row 18: K2, P8, TL, P5, TR, P8, K2,

Row 19: K 11, P1, K5, P1, K 11.

Row 20: K2, P9, TL, P3, TR, P9, K2.

Row 21: K 12, P1, K3, P1, K 12.

Row 22: K2, P 10, TL, P1, TR, P 10, K2.

Row 23: K 13, P1, K1, P1, K 13.

Row 24: K2, P 11, slip next 2 sts onto cable needle and hold in **back** of work, K1 from left needle, (P1, K1) from cable needle, P 11, K2.

Row 25: K 13, P1, K1, P1, K 13.

Row 26: K2, P 10, TR, P1, TL, P 10, K2.

Row 27: K 12, P1, K3, P1, K 12.

Row 28: K2, P9, TR, P3, TL, P9, K2.

Row 29: K 11, P1, K5, P1, K 11.

Row 30: K2, P8, TR, P5, TL, P8, K2.

Row 31: K 10, P1, K7, P1, K 10.

Row 32: K2, P8, K1, P7, K1, P8, K2.

Rows 33-35: Repeat Rows 31 and 32 once, then repeat Row 31 once **more**.

Row 36: K2, P8, TL, P5, TR, P8, K2.

Row 37: K 11, P1, K5, P1, K 11.

Row 38: K2, P9, TL, P3, TR, P9, K2.

Row 39: K 12, M1, P1, K3 tog, P1, M1, K 12.

Row 40: K2, P 11, slip next 2 sts onto cable needle and hold in **back** of work, P1 from left needle, P2 from cable needle, P 11, K2.

Rows 41-49: Repeat Rows 1 and 2, 4 times; then repeat Row 1 once **more**.

Bind off all sts in pattern.

FINISHING
Spray with starch and press flat on wrong side. Insert in window opening of card, use dots of glue under frame edge to hold in place; let dry. ♥

ENTRELAC PILLOW

A gift of comfort that's pretty in pink, this pillow will remind her that you care.

◼◻◻◻ EASY +

Finished Measurement: 18" (45.5 cm) square

MATERIALS

Medium Weight Yarn **4** MEDIUM
[4 ounces, 203 yards
(113 grams, 186 meters) per skein]:
3 skeins
24" (61 cm) Circular knitting needle,
size 10½ (6.5 mm) **or** size needed
for gauge
Markers (at least one contrasting color)
18" (45.5 cm) Square pillow
Yarn needle

GAUGE: With 2 strands of yarn held
together, in Stockinette Stitch,
12 sts and 18 rows = 4" (10 cm)

Techniques used:
- YO (*Fig. 4a, page 89*)
- K2 tog (*Fig. 7, page 91*)
- P2 tog (*Fig. 8, page 91*)
- SSK (*Figs. 9a-c, page 91*)
- Slip 1 as if to **knit**, K2 tog, PSSO
  (*Figs. 12a & b, page 92*)
- Slip 2 tog as if to **knit**, K1, P2SSO
  (*Figs. 13a & b, page 93*)

PILLOW FRONT
SQUARE #1

With 2 strands of yarn held together, cast on 15 sts.

Set-Up Row: Purl across.

Row 1 (Right side)**:** K 15.

Row 2 AND ALL WRONG SIDE ROWS: P 15.

Row 3: K 15.

Row 5: K4, YO, SSK, K3, K2 tog, YO, K4.

Row 7: K5, YO, SSK, K1, K2 tog, YO, K5.

Row 9: K6, YO, slip 1 as if to **knit**, K2 tog, PSSO, YO, K6.

Row 11: K6, K2 tog, YO, K7.

Row 13: K5, K2 tog, YO, K1, YO, SSK, K5.

Rows 15, 17 and 19: K4, K2 tog, YO, K3, YO, SSK, K4.

Row 21: K6, YO, slip 2 tog as if to **knit**, K1, P2SSO, YO, K6.

Rows 23-28: Repeat Rows 1 and 2, 3 times.

Do **not** cut yarn.

PILLOW FRONT DIAGRAM

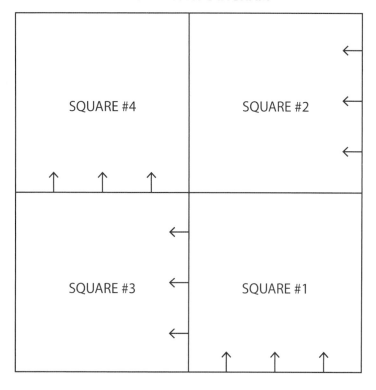

Arrows indicate knitting direction for each Square.

SQUARE #2

With **right** side facing, cast on 15 sts using backward loop method *(Fig. 2, page 89)*: 30 sts.

Set-Up Row: K 14, SSK (uses last st of cast on and one st from Square #1); leave remaining 14 sts of Square #1 unworked: 15 sts on right needle tip.

Row 1 AND ALL WRONG SIDE ROWS: Slip 1 as if to **purl**, P 14.

Row 2: K 14, SSK (uses one st from Square #1); leave remaining 13 sts of Square #1 unworked.

Row 4: K 14, SSK (uses one st from Square #1); leave remaining 12 sts of Square #1 unworked.

Row 6: K4, YO, SSK, K3, K2 tog, YO, K3, SSK (uses one st from Square #1); leave remaining 11 sts of Square #1 unworked.

Row 8: K5, YO, SSK, K1, K2 tog, YO, K4, SSK (uses one st from Square #1); leave remaining 10 sts of Square #1 unworked.

Row 10: K6, YO, slip 1 as if to **knit**, K2 tog, PSSO, YO, K5, SSK (uses one st from Square #1); leave remaining 9 sts of Square #1 unworked.

Row 12: K6, K2 tog, YO, K6, SSK (uses one st from Square #1); leave remaining 8 sts of Square #1 unworked.

Row 14: K5, K2 tog, YO, K1, YO, SSK, K4, SSK (uses one st from Square #1); leave remaining 7 sts of Square #1 unworked.

Rows 16, 18 and 20: K4, K2 tog, YO, K3, YO, SSK, K3, SSK (uses one st from Square #1); leave remaining sts of Square #1 unworked.

Row 22: K6, YO, slip 2 tog as if to **knit**, K1, P2SSO, YO, K5, SK (uses one st from Square #1); leave remaining 3 sts of Square #1 unworked.

Rows 24 and 26: K 14, SSK (uses one st from Square #1); leave remaining st(s) of Square #1 unworked.

Row 28: K 14, SSK (uses last st from Square #1); do **not** cut yarn: 15 sts.

SQUARE #3

With **right** side facing, pick up 15 sts evenly spaced across end of rows on Square #1 *(Fig. 14a, page 93)*: 15 sts on Square #2 **and** 15 sts on Square #3.

Set-Up Row: P 15, leave remaining 15 sts from Square #2 unworked.

Rows 1-27: Work same as Square #1, page 62, leaving sts from Square #2 unworked.

Bind off all sts **loosely** in **purl**, leaving last st on right needle tip; do **not** cut yarn.

SQUARE #4

With **wrong** side facing and last st from Square #3 on right needle tip, pick up 14 sts evenly spaced across end of rows on Square #3 [these sts will be picked up **purlwise**, since they are picked up from the **back** side of the work *(Fig. 14c, page 93)*], slip last st picked up onto left needle tip and P2 tog with first st from Square #2: 15 sts on Square #4 **and** 14 sts on Square #2.

Row 1: Slip 1 as if to **purl**, K 14.

Row 2: P 14, P2 tog (uses one st from Square #2); leave remaining 13 sts of Square #2 unworked.

Row 3: Slip 1 as if to **purl**, K 14.

Row 4: P 14, P2 tog (uses one st from Square #2); leave remaining 12 sts of Square #2 unworked.

Row 5: Slip 1 as if to **purl**, K3, YO, SSK, K3, K2 tog, YO, K4.

Row 6: P 14, P2 tog (uses one st from Square #2); leave remaining 11 sts of Square #2 unworked.

Row 7: Slip 1 as if to **purl**, K4, YO, SSK, K1, K2 tog, YO, K5.

Row 8: P 14, P2 tog (uses one st from Square #2); leave remaining 10 sts of Square #2 unworked.

Row 9: Slip 1 as if to **purl**, K5, YO, slip 1 as if to **knit**, K2 tog, PSSO, YO, K6.

Row 10: P 14, P2 tog (uses one st from Square #2); leave remaining 9 sts of Square #2 unworked.

Row 11: Slip 1 as if to **purl**, K5, K2 tog, YO, K7.

Row 12: P 14, P2 tog (uses one st from Square #2); leave remaining 8 sts of Square #2 unworked.

Row 13: Slip 1 as if to **purl**, K4, K2 tog, YO, K1, YO, SSK, K5.

Row 14: P 14, P2 tog (uses one st from Square #2); leave remaining 7 sts of Square #2 unworked.

Row 15: Slip 1 as if to **purl**, K3, K2 tog, YO, K3, YO, SSK, K4.

Row 16: P 14, P2 tog (uses one st from Square #2); leave remaining sts of Square #2 unworked.

Rows 17-20: Repeat Rows 15 and 16 twice.

Row 21: Slip 1 as if to **purl**, K5, YO, slip 2 tog as if to **knit**, K1, P2SSO, YO, K6.

Row 22: P 14, P2 tog (uses one st from Square #2); leave remaining 3 sts of Square #2 unworked.

Row 23: Slip 1 as if to **purl**, K 14.

Row 24: P 14, P2 tog (uses one st from Square #2); leave remaining st(s) of Square #2 unworked.

Rows 25-27: Repeat Rows 23 and 24 once, then repeat Row 23 once **more**.

Row 28: P 14, P2 tog (uses last st from Square #2).

Slipping the first st as if to **knit**, bind off all sts **very loosely** in **knit**, leaving last st on needle; do **not** cut yarn.

BORDER

Helpful Hint: When picking up sts along Entrelac Squares, pick up 19 sts evenly spaced across end of rows and 14 sts evenly spaced along the bottom and top of the Squares *(Fig. 14b, page 93)*, placing markers as indicated *(see Markers, page 87)*.

With **right** side facing and last st from Square #4 on right needle tip, pick up 32 sts evenly spaced across the side of Entrelac Squares, ★ place marker, pick up 33 sts evenly spaced across next edge of Entrelac Squares; repeat from ★ 2 times **more**, place a contrasting color marker to mark the beginning of the round: 132 sts.

Rnd 1: ★ K1, YO, knit across to next marker, YO, slip marker; repeat from ★ around: 140 sts.

Rnd 2: Knit around, slipping markers.

Rnds 3-10: Repeat Rnds 1 and 2, 4 times: 172 sts.

Bind Off Row: Remove first marker, K1, replace marker, bind off next 128 sts **very loosely** in **knit**, K 21, K2 tog, knit across remaining sts; do **not** cut yarn: 43 sts.

PILLOW BACK

Row 1: Purl across.

Row 2: Knit across.

Rows 3-17: Repeat Rows 1 and 2, 7 times; then repeat Row 1 once **more**.

Row 18: K 17, YO, SSK, K5, K2 tog, YO, K 17.

Row 19 AND ALL WRONG SIDE ROWS: Purl across.

Row 20: K 18, YO, SSK, K3, K2 tog, YO, K 18.

Row 22: K 19, YO, SSK, K1, K2 tog, YO, K 19.

Row 24: K 20, YO, slip 1 as if to **knit**, K2 tog, PSSO, YO, K 20.

Row 26: K 20, K2 tog, YO, K 21.

Row 28: K 19, K2 tog, YO, K1, YO, SSK, K 19.

Row 30: K 18, K2 tog, YO, K3, YO, SSK, K 18.

Row 32: K 17, K2 tog, YO, K5, YO, SSK, K 17.

Rows 34-39: Repeat Rows 32 and 33, 3 times.

Row 40: K 19, YO, SSK, K1, K2 tog, YO, K 19.

Row 42: K 20, YO, slip 2 tog as if to **knit**, K1, P2SSO, YO, K 20.

Rows 43-62: Repeat Rows 1 and 2, 10 times.

Bind off all sts **loosely** in **purl**, leaving a long end for sewing.

FINISHING

Thread yarn needle with long end.
With **wrong** side together, sew top and one side.
Insert pillow and sew remaining side. 💙

HOT WATER BOTTLE COVER

Convey your thoughts and prayers with a little extra warmth!

EASY

Finished Measurements:

8¼" wide x 13" long (21 cm x 33 cm) (flattened) [includes 3" (7.5 cm) ribbing for the neck of the hot water bottle] , to fit a standard hot water bottle measuring 7¼" wide x 10" long (18.5 cm x 25.5 cm)

MATERIALS

Bulky Weight Yarn **(5 BULKY)**
[3.5 ounces, 136 yards
(100 grams, 124 meters) per skein]:
   One skein
16" (40.5 cm) Circular knitting needle,
   size 9 (5.5 mm) **or** size needed for gauge
Cable needle
Markers (at least one contrasting color)
Yarn needle

GAUGE: In Stockinette Stitch,
       16 sts and 22 rows = 4" (10 cm)

Techniques used:

• YO **(Figs. 4b & d, pages 89 & 90)**
• M1P **(Fig. 6, page 90)**
• P2 tog **(Fig. 8, page 91)**
• P3 tog **(Fig. 11, page 92)**

STITCH GUIDE

CROSS RIGHT (*abbreviated CR*) (uses 2 sts)
Knit into the **front** of the second st on the left needle, then **knit** the first st, letting both sts drop off the needle at the same time.

TWIST LEFT (*abbreviated TL*) (uses 2 sts)
Slip next st onto cable needle and hold in **front** of work, P1 from left needle, K1 from cable needle.

TWIST RIGHT (*abbreviated TR*) (uses 2 sts)
Knit into the **front** of the second st on the left needle, then **purl** the first st, letting both sts drop off the needle at the same time.

BODY

Leaving an 18" (45.5 cm) length for sewing, cast on 27 sts (front), place a marker to denote the side **(see Markers, page 87)**, cast on 27 additional sts (back); being careful not to twist sts on needle, place a contrasting color marker to mark the beginning of the rnd: 54 sts.

Each round of instructions is worked across the front and the back. Slip the side marker before repeating the instructions across the back sts.

Rnds 1 and 2 (Right side): ★ P1, K2, P 21, K2, P1; repeat from ★ once **more**.

Rnd 3: ★ P1, M1P, K2, P 21, K2, M1P, P1; repeat from ★ once **more**: 58 sts.

Rnd 4: ★ P2, CR, P 21, CR, P2; repeat from ★ once **more**.

Rnds 5 and 6: ★ P2, K2, P 21, K2, P2; repeat from ★ once **more**.

Rnd 7: ★ P1, M1P, P1, K2, P 21, K2, P1, M1P, P1; repeat from ★ once **more**: 62 sts.

Rnd 8: ★ P3, CR, P 21, CR, P3; repeat from ★ once **more**.

Rnds 9 and 10: ★ P3, K2, P 21, K2, P3; repeat from ★ once **more**.

Rnd 11: ★ P2, M1P, P1, K2, P 21, K2, P1, M1P, P2; repeat from ★ once **more**: 66 sts.

Rnd 12: ★ P4, CR, P 21, CR, P4; repeat from ★ once **more**.

Rnds 13 and 14: ★ P4, K2, P 21, K2, P4; repeat from ★ once **more**.

Rnd 15: ★ P4, K2, P 14, K1, P6, K2, P4; repeat from ★ once **more**.

Rnd 16: ★ P4, CR, P 14, K1, P6, CR, P4; repeat from ★ once **more**.

Rnd 17: ★ P4, K2, P 14, K1, P6, K2, P4; repeat from ★ once **more**.

Rnds 18 and 19: ★ P4, K2, P6, K1, P7, K1, P6, K2, P4; repeat from ★ once **more**.

Rnd 20: ★ P4, CR, P6, K1, P7, K1, P6, CR, P4; repeat from ★ once **more**.

Rnds 21 and 22: ★ P4, K2, P6, K1, P7, K1, P6, K2, P4; repeat from ★ once **more**.

Rnd 23: ★ P4, K2, P6, TL, P5, TR, P6, K2, P4; repeat from ★ once **more**.

Rnd 24: ★ P4, CR, P7, K1, P5, K1, P7, CR, P4; repeat from ★ once **more**.

Rnd 25: ★ P4, K2, P7, TL, P3, TR, P7, K2, P4; repeat from ★ once **more**.

Rnd 26: ★ P4, K2, P8, K1, P3, K1, P8, K2, P4; repeat from ★ once **more**.

Rnd 27: ★ P4, K2, P8, TL, P1, TR, P8, K2, P4; repeat from ★ once **more**.

Rnd 28: ★ P4, CR, P9, K1, P1, K1, P9, CR, P4; repeat from ★ once **more**.

Rnd 29: ★ P4, K2, P9, slip next 2 sts onto cable needle and hold in **back** of work, K1 from left needle, (P1, K1) from cable needle, P9, K2, P4; repeat from ★ once **more**.

Rnd 30: ★ P4, K2, P9, K1, P1, K1, P9, K2, P4; repeat from ★ once **more**.

Rnd 31: ★ P4, K2, P8, TR, P1, TL, P8, K2, P4; repeat from ★ once **more**.

Rnd 32: ★ P4, CR, P8, K1, P3, K1, P8, CR, P4; repeat from ★ once **more**.

Rnd 33: ★ P4, K2, P7, TR, P3, TL, P7, K2, P4; repeat from ★ once **more**.

Rnd 34: ★ P4, K2, P7, K1, P5, K1, P7, K2, P4; repeat from ★ once **more**.

Rnd 35: ★ P4, K2, P6, TR, P5, TL, P6, K2, P4; repeat from ★ once **more**.

Rnd 36: ★ P4, CR, P6, K1, P7, K1, P6, CR, P4; repeat from ★ once **more**.

Rnds 37-39: ★ P4, K2, P6, K1, P7, K1, P6, K2, P4; repeat from ★ once **more**.

Rnd 40: ★ P4, CR, P6, K1, P7, K1, P6, CR, P4; repeat from ★ once **more**.

Rnd 41: ★ P4, K2, P6, TL, P5, TR, P6, K2, P4; repeat from ★ once **more**.

Rnd 42: ★ P4, K2, P7, K1, P5, K1, P7, K2, P4; repeat from ★ once **more**.

Rnd 43: ★ P4, K2, P7, TL, P3, TR, P7, K2, P4; repeat from ★ once **more**.

Rnd 44: ★ P4, CR, P8, M1P, K1, P3 tog, K1, M1P, P8, CR, P4; repeat from ★ once **more**.

Rnd 45: ★ P4, K2, P9, slip next 2 sts onto cable needle and hold in **back** of work, P1 from left needle, P2 from cable needle, P9, K2, P4; repeat from ★ once **more**.

Rnds 46 and 47: ★ P4, K2, P 21, K2, P4; repeat from ★ once **more**.

Rnd 48: ★ P4, CR, P 21, CR, P4; repeat from ★ once **more**.

Rnds 49-51: ★ P4, K2, P 21, K2, P4; repeat from ★ once **more**.

Rnds 52-56: Repeat Rnds 48-51 once, then repeat Row 48 once **more**.

BOTTLE NECK

Rnd 1 (Decrease rnd)**:** ★ P2 tog twice, K2, P2, K2, (P2 tog, P1, K2) 3 times, P2, K2, P2 tog twice; repeat from ★ once **more**: 52 sts.

Rnds 2 and 3: ★ P2, (K2, P2) across to marker; repeat from ★ once **more**.

Rnd 4: ★ P2, (CR, P2) across to marker; repeat from ★ once **more**.

Rnds 5-7: ★ P2, (K2, P2) across to marker; repeat from ★ once **more**.

Rnd 8 (Eyelet rnd)**:** ★ P2 tog, YO, (CR, P2 tog, YO) across to marker; repeat from ★ once **more**.

Rnds 9-11: ★ P2, (K2, P2) across to marker; repeat from ★ once **more**.

Rnd 12: ★ P2, (CR, P2) across to marker; repeat from ★ once **more**.

Rnds 13-15: ★ P2, (K2, P2) across to marker; repeat from ★ once **more**.

Bind off remaining sts in pattern.

FINISHING

Sew bottom seam, matching sts and cables carefully.

Tie: Make a 32" (81.5 cm) twisted cord *(see Twisted Cord, page 93)*.

Weave Tie through YO's on Eyelet round and tie in a bow at center front. 🖤

LAP THROW

This is a just-right wrap for everyday use—one that isn't too heavy or too long.

◼◼▢▢ **EASY**

Finished Measurement:
43³/₄" wide x 49" long (111 cm x 124.5 cm)

MATERIALS

Medium Weight Yarn MEDIUM ④
[3.5 ounces, 207 yards
(100 grams, 188 meters) per skein]:
    7 skeins
29" (73.5 cm) Circular knitting needle,
    size 9 (5.5 mm) **or** size needed for gauge
Markers - 9

GAUGE: In Stockinette Stitch,
                16 sts and 22 rows = 4" (10 cm)

Techniques used:

• YO *(Fig. 4a, page 89)*
• K2 tog *(Fig. 7, page 91)*
• SSK *(Figs. 9a-c, page 91)*
• Slip 1 as if to **knit**, K2 tog, PSSO
  (Figs. 12a & b, page 92)
• Slip 2 tog as if to **knit**, K1, P2SSO
  (Figs. 13a & b, page 93)

THROW
BOTTOM BORDER
Cast on 175 sts.

Rows 1-5: Knit across (Garter Stitch).

BODY
Row 1(Right side)**:** ★ K 19, place marker *(see Markers, page 87)*; repeat from ★ across to last 4 sts, K4.

Row 2 AND ALL WRONG SIDE ROWS THROUGH Row 24: K4, ★ slip marker, P 15, K4; repeat from ★ across.

Row 3: Knit across slipping markers.

Row 5: ★ K8, YO, SSK, K3, K2 tog, YO, K4, slip marker; repeat from ★ across to last 4 sts, K4.

Row 7: ★ K9, YO, SSK, K1, K2 tog, YO, K5, slip marker; repeat from ★ across to last 4 sts, K4.

Row 9: ★ K 10, YO, slip 1 as if to **knit**, K2 tog, PSSO, YO, K6, slip marker; repeat from ★ across to last 4 sts, K4.

Row 11: ★ K 10, K2 tog, YO, K7, slip marker; repeat from ★ across to last 4 sts, K4.

Row 13: ★ K9, K2 tog, YO, K1, YO, SSK, K5, slip marker; repeat from ★ across to last 4 sts, K4.

Row 15: ★ K8, K2 tog, YO, K3, YO, SSK, K4, slip marker; repeat from ★ across to last 4 sts, K4.

Rows 16-22: Repeat Rows 14 and 15, 3 times; then repeat Row 14 once **more**.

Row 23: ★ K 10, YO, slip 2 tog as if to **knit**, K1, P2SSO, YO, K6, slip marker; repeat from ★ across to last 4 sts, K4.

Rows 25-31: Knit across slipping markers.

Row 32 AND ALL WRONG SIDE ROWS THROUGH Row 54: K4, ★ slip marker, P 15, K4; repeat from ★ across.

Row 33: Knit across slipping markers.

Row 35: K8, YO, SSK, K3, K2 tog, YO, K4, slip marker, (K 19, slip marker) 7 times, K8, YO, SSK, K3, K2 tog, YO, K8.

Row 37: K9, YO, SSK, K1, K2 tog, YO, K5, slip marker, (K 19, slip marker) 7 times, K9, YO, SSK, K1, K2 tog, YO, K9.

Row 39: K 10, YO, slip 1 as if to **knit**, K2 tog, PSSO, YO, K6, slip marker, (K 19, slip marker) 7 times, K 10, YO, slip 1 as if to **knit**, K2 tog, PSSO, YO, K 10.

Row 41: K 10, K2 tog, YO, K7, slip marker, (K 19, slip marker) 7 times, K 10, K2 tog, YO, K 11.

Row 43: K9, K2 tog, YO, K1, YO, SSK, K5, slip marker, (K 19, slip marker) 7 times, K9, K2 tog, YO, K1, YO, SSK K9.

Row 45: K8, K2 tog, YO, K3, YO, SSK, K4, slip marker, (K 19, slip marker) 7 times, K8, K2 tog, YO, K3, YO, SSK, K8.

Rows 46-52: Repeat Rows 44 and 45, 3 times; then repeat Row 44 once **more**.

Row 53: K 10, YO, slip 2 tog as if to **knit**, K1, P2SSO, YO, K6, slip marker, (K 19, slip marker) 7 times, K 10, YO, slip 2 tog as if to **knit**, K1, P2SSO, YO, K 10.

Rows 55-61: Knit across slipping markers.

Row 62 AND ALL WRONG SIDE ROWS THROUGH Row 84: K4, ★ slip marker, P 15, K4; repeat from ★ across.

Row 63: Knit across slipping markers.

Row 65: K8, YO, SSK, K3, K2 tog, YO, K4, slip marker, K 19, slip marker, ★ K8, YO, SSK, K3, K2 tog, YO, K4, slip marker; repeat from ★ 4 times **more**, K 19, slip marker, K8, YO, SSK, K3, K2 tog, YO, K8.

Row 67: K9, YO, SSK, K1, K2 tog, YO, K5, slip marker, K 19, slip marker, ★ K9, YO, SSK, K1, K2 tog, YO, K5, slip marker; repeat from ★ 4 times **more**, K 19, slip marker, K9, YO, SSK, K1, K2 tog, YO, K9.

Row 69: K 10, YO, slip 1 as if to **knit**, K2 tog, PSSO, YO, K6, slip marker, K 19, slip marker, ★ K 10, YO, slip 1 as if to **knit**, K2 tog, PSSO, YO, K6, slip marker; repeat from ★ 4 times **more**, K 19, slip marker, K 10, YO, slip 1 as if to **knit**, K2 tog, PSSO, YO, K 10.

Row 71: K 10, K2 tog, YO, K7, slip marker, K 19, slip marker, ★ K 10, K2 tog, YO, K7, slip marker; repeat from ★ 4 times **more**, K 19, slip marker, K 10, K2 tog, YO, K 11.

Row 73: K9, K2 tog, YO, K1, YO, SSK, K5, slip marker, K 19, slip marker, ★ K9, K2 tog, YO, K1, YO, SSK, K5, slip marker; repeat from ★ 4 times **more**, K 19, slip marker, K9, K2 tog, YO, K1, YO, SSK, K9.

Row 75: K8, K2 tog, YO, K3, YO, SSK, K4, slip marker, K 19, slip marker, ★ K8, K2 tog, YO, K3, YO, SSK, K4, slip marker; repeat from ★ 4 times **more**, K 19, slip marker, K8, K2 tog, YO, K3, YO, SSK, K8.

Rows 76-82: Repeat Rows 74 and 75, 3 times; then repeat Row 74 once **more**.

Row 83: K 10, YO, slip 2 tog as if to **knit**, K1, P2SSO, YO, K6, slip marker, K 19, slip marker, ★ K 10, YO, slip 2 tog as if to **knit**, K1, P2SSO, YO, K6, slip marker; repeat from ★ 4 times **more**, K 19, slip marker, K 10, YO, slip 2 tog as if to **knit**, K1, P2SSO, YO, K 10.

Rows 85-91: Knit across slipping markers.

Row 92 AND ALL WRONG SIDE ROWS THROUGH Row 114: K4, ★ slip marker, P 15, K4; repeat from ★ across.

Row 93: Knit across slipping markers.

Row 95: † K8, YO, SSK, K3, K2 tog, YO, K4, slip marker, K 19, slip marker, K8, YO, SSK, K3, K2 tog, YO, K4, slip marker †, (K 19, slip marker) 3 times, repeat from † to † once, K4.

Row 97: † K9, YO, SSK, K1, K2 tog, YO, K5, slip marker, K 19, slip marker, K9, YO, SSK, K1, K2 tog, YO, K5, slip marker †, (K 19, slip marker) 3 times, repeat from † to † once, K4.

Row 99: † K 10, YO, slip 1 as if to **knit**, K2 tog, PSSO, YO, K6, slip marker, K 19, slip marker, K 10, YO, slip 1 as if to **knit**, K2 tog, PSSO, YO, K6, slip marker †, (K 19, slip marker) 3 times, repeat from † to † once, K4.

Row 101: † K 10, K2 tog, YO, K7, slip marker, K 19, slip marker, K 10, K2 tog, YO, K7, slip marker †, (K 19, slip marker) 3 times, repeat from † to † once, K4.

Row 103: † K9, K2 tog, YO, K1, YO, SSK, K5, slip marker, K 19, slip marker, K9, K2 tog, YO, K1, YO, SSK, K5, slip marker †, (K 19, slip marker) 3 times, repeat from † to † once, K4.

Row 105: † K8, K2 tog, YO, K3, YO, SSK, K4, slip marker, K 19, slip marker, K8, K2 tog, YO, K3, YO, SSK, K4, slip marker †, (K 19, slip marker) 3 times, repeat from † to † once, K4.

Rows 106-112: Repeat Rows 104 and 105, 3 times; then repeat Row 104 once **more**.

Row 113: † K 10, YO, slip 2 tog as if to **knit**, K1, P2SSO, YO, K6, slip marker, K 19, slip marker, K 10, YO, slip 2 tog as if to **knit**, K1, P2SSO, YO, K6, slip marker †, (K 19, slip marker) 3 times, repeat from † to † once, K4.

Rows 115-121: Knit across slipping markers.

Row 122 AND ALL WRONG SIDE ROWS THROUGH Row 144: K4, ★ slip marker, P 15, K4; repeat from ★ across.

Row 123: Knit across slipping markers.

Row 125: ★ K8, YO, SSK, K3, K2 tog, YO, K4, slip marker, K 19, slip marker; repeat from ★ 3 times **more**, K8, YO, SSK, K3, K2 tog, YO, K8.

Row 127: ★ K9, YO, SSK, K1, K2 tog, YO, K5, slip marker, K 19, slip marker; repeat from ★ 3 times **more**, K9, YO, SSK, K1, K2 tog, YO, K9.

Row 129: ★ K 10, YO, slip 1 as if to **knit**, K2 tog, PSSO, YO, K6, slip marker, K 19, slip marker; repeat from ★ 3 times **more**, K 10, YO, slip 1 as if to **knit**, K2 tog, PSSO, YO, K 10.

Row 131: ★ K 10, K2 tog, YO, K7, slip marker, K 19, slip marker; repeat from ★ 3 times **more**, K 10, K2 tog, YO, K 11.

Row 133: ★ K9, K2 tog, YO, K1, YO, SSK, K5, slip marker, K 19, slip marker; repeat from ★ 3 times **more**, K9, K2 tog, YO, K1, YO, SSK, K9.

Row 135: ★ K8, K2 tog, YO, K3, YO, SSK, K4, slip marker, K 19, slip marker; repeat from ★ 3 times **more**, K8, K2 tog, YO, K3, YO, SSK, K8.

Rows 136-142: Repeat Rows 134 and 135, 3 times; then repeat Row 134 once **more**.

Row 143: ★ K 10, YO, slip 2 tog as if to **knit**, K1, P2SSO, YO, K6, slip marker, K 19, slip marker; repeat from ★ 3 times **more**, K 10, YO, slip 2 tog as if to **knit**, K1, P2SSO, YO, K 10.

Rows 145-151: Knit across slipping markers.

Rows 152-181: Repeat Rows 92-121.

Rows 182-211: Repeat Rows 62-91.

Rows 212-241: Repeat Rows 32-61.

Rows 242-263: Repeat Rows 2-23.

Row 264: K4, ★ remove marker, P 15, K4; repeat from ★ across.

TOP BORDER
Rows 1-6: Knit across.

Bind off all sts in **knit**. 🖤

MUG COZY

A thermal mug cozy is fun to present with a box of gourmet hot chocolate mixes or flavored coffees. It's a gift that can warm the heart.

■□□□ **EASY**

Finished Measurement:
  3" wide x 9" long (7.5 cm x 23 cm)

MATERIALS

Medium Weight Yarn
[1.75 ounces, 109 yards
(50 grams, 100 grams) per ball]:
  One ball [approximately 40 yards (36.5 meters)]
Straight knitting needles, size 7 (4.5 mm) **or**
  size needed for gauge
Cable needle
Yarn needle

GAUGE: In Stockinette Stitch,
            20 sts and 26 rows = 4" (10 cm)

Techniques used:
- M1 *(Figs. 5a & b, page 90)*
- K3 tog *(Fig. 10, page 92)*

STITCH GUIDE

CROSS RIGHT *(abbreviated CR)* (uses 2 sts)
Knit into the **front** of the second st on the left needle, then **knit** the first st, letting both sts drop off the needle at the same time.
TWIST LEFT *(abbreviated TL)* (uses 2 sts)
Slip next st onto cable needle and hold in **front** of work, P1 from left needle, K1 from cable needle.
TWIST RIGHT *(abbreviated TR)* (uses 2 sts)
Knit into the **front** of the second st on the left needle, then **purl** the first st, letting both sts drop off the needle at the same time.

COZY

Cast on 19 sts.

Row 1: K2, P2, K 11, P2, K2.

Row 2 (Right side)**:** K4, P 11, K4.

Row 3: K2, P2, K 11, P2, K2.

Row 4: K2, CR, P 11, CR, K2.

Row 5: K2, P2, K2, P1, K8, P2, K2.

Row 6: K4, P8, K1, P2, K4.

Row 7: K2, P2, K2, P1, K5, P1, K2, P2, K2.

Row 8: K2, CR, P2, K1, P5, K1, P2, CR, K2.

Row 9: K2, P2, K2, P1, K5, P1, K2, P2, K2.

Row 10: K4, P2, K1, P5, K1, P2, K4.

Row 11: K2, P2, K2, P1, K5, P1, K2, P2, K2.

Row 12: K2, CR, P2, TL, P3, TR, P2, CR, K2.

Row 13: K2, P2, K3, (P1, K3) twice, P2, K2.

Row 14: K4, P3, TL, P1, TR, P3, K4.

Row 15: K2, P2, K4, P1, K1, P1, K4, P2, K2.

Row 16: K2, CR, P4, slip next 2 sts onto cable needle and hold in **back** of work, K1 from left needle, (P1, K1) from cable needle, P4, CR, K2.

Row 17: K2, P2, K4, P1, K1, P1, K4, P2, K2.

Row 18: K4, P3, TR, P1, TL, P3, K4.

Row 19: K2, P2, K3, (P1, K3) twice, P2, K2.

Row 20: K2, CR, P2, TR, P3, TL, P2, CR, K2.

Row 21: K2, P2, K2, P1, K5, P1, K2, P2, K2.

Row 22: K4, P2, K1, P5, K1, P2, K4.

Row 23: K2, P2, K2, P1, K5, P1, K2, P2, K2.

Row 24: K2, CR, P2, K1, P5, K1, P2, CR, K2.

Row 25: K2, P2, K2, P1, K5, P1, K2, P2, K2.

Row 26: K4, P2, TL, P3, TR, P2, K4.

Row 27: K2, P2, K3, M1, P1, K3 tog, P1, M1, K3, P2, K2.

Row 28: K2, CR, P4, slip next 2 sts onto cable needle and hold in **back** of work, P1 from left needle, P2 from cable needle, P4, CR, K2.

Rows 29-32: Repeat Rows 1-4.

Cozy needs to be smaller than the mug, so that it fits around mug snugly and does not fall off. Measure around your thermal mug; then measure the length of your Cozy and multiply it by 2. If it needs to be a little longer, repeat Rows 1-4 once **more**. If not, then continue with remaining rows.

Rows 33-59: Repeat Rows 5-31.

Bind off all sts in pattern, leaving a long end for sewing.

Thread yarn needle with long end. Matching sts, sew short ends together. ♥

SACHET OR SOAP COVER

Make two and fill one with a lavender sachet bag and the other with a bar of luxury soap. It's a fragrant gift idea to go with the Face Cloth on page 56.

EASY

Finished Measurement:
    7" circumference x 6" tall (18 cm x 15 cm)

MATERIALS
Light Weight Yarn
[1³/₄ ounces, 110 yards
(50 grams, 100 meters) per skein]:
    One skein [approximately 35 yards (32 meters)
    for **each** Cover]
Straight knitting needles, size 7 (4.5 mm) **or**
    size needed for gauge
Tapestry needle
³/₈" (10 mm) Ribbon - 12" (30.5 cm) length

GAUGE: In Stockinette Stitch,
            20 sts and 28 rows = 4" (10 cm)

Techniques used:
* YO (**Fig. 4a, page 89**)
* K2 tog (**Fig. 7, page 91**)
* SSK (**Figs. 9a-c, page 91**)
* Slip 1 as if to **knit**, K2 tog, PSSO
    (**Figs. 12a & b, page 92**)
* Slip 2 tog as if to **knit**, K1, P2SSO
    (**Figs. 13a & b, page 93**)

COVER
Cast 37 sts.

Set-Up Row: Purl across.

Row 1 (Right side)**:** Knit across.

Row 2: Purl across.

Rows 3-8: Repeat Rows 1 and 2, 3 times.

Row 9: K6, YO, SSK, K3, K2 tog, YO, K 11, YO, SSK, K3, K2 tog, YO, K6.

Row 10: Purl across.

Row 11: K7, YO, SSK, K1, K2 tog, YO, K 13, YO, SSK, K1, K2 tog, YO, K7.

Row 12: Purl across.

Row 13: K8, YO, slip 1 as if to **knit**, K2 tog, PSSO, YO, K 15, YO, slip 1 as if to **knit**, K2 tog, PSSO, YO, K8.

Row 14: Purl across.

Row 15: K8, K2 tog, YO, K 16, YO, K2 tog, K9.

Row 16: Purl across.

Row 17: K7, K2 tog, YO, K1, YO, SSK, K 13, K2 tog, YO, K1, YO, SSK, K7.

Row 18: Purl across.

Row 19: K6, K2 tog, YO, K3, YO, SSK, K 11, K2 tog, YO, K3, YO, SSK, K6.

Row 20: Purl across.

Rows 21-24: Repeat Rows 19 and 20 twice.

Row 25: K8, YO, slip 2 tog as if to **knit**, K1, P2SSO, YO, K 15, YO, slip 2 tog as if to **knit**, K1, P2SSO, YO, K8.

Row 26: Purl across.

Rows 27-34: Repeat Rows 1 and 2, 4 times.

Row 35: K1, (K2 tog, YO, K1, YO, SSK) across to last st, K1.

Row 36: Purl across.

Rows 37-41: Repeat Rows 35 and 36 twice, then repeat Row 35 once **more**.

Bind off all sts in **knit**, leaving a long end for sewing.

FINISHING

Thread tapestry needle with long end.
With **right** side together and matching rows, sew end of rows together for side seam, then sew bottom seam. Turn piece right side out.

Insert a handmade bar of soap or a bag of lavender for a sachet.

Beginning at center front, weave ribbon through YO's on Row 35; tie in a bow. ♥

TEAPOT COZY

A Teapot Cozy is a such a thoughtful gift, especially when presented with a teapot and a tin of gourmet tea.

 EASY

Finished Measurement:
19¹/₂" circumference x 8" tall (49.5 cm x 20.5 cm)

MATERIALS
Medium Weight Yarn
[1.75 ounces, 109 yards
(50 grams, 100 grams) per ball]:
   2 balls
Straight knitting needles, size 7 (4.5 mm) **or**
   size needed for gauge
Cable needle
Yarn needle

GAUGE: In Stockinette Stitch,
20 sts and 26 rows = 4" (10 cm)

Techniques used:
* YO *(Fig. 4a, page 89)*
* M1 *(Figs. 5a & b, page 90)*
* K2 tog *(Fig. 7, page 91)*
* K3 tog *(Fig. 10, page 92)*

STITCH GUIDE
CROSS RIGHT *(abbreviated CR)* (uses 2 sts)
Knit into the **front** of the second st on the left needle, then **knit** the first st, letting both sts drop off the needle at the same time.
TWIST LEFT *(abbreviated TL)* (uses 2 sts)
Slip next st onto cable needle and hold in **front** of work, P1 from left needle, K1 from cable needle.
TWIST RIGHT *(abbreviated TR)* (uses 2 sts)
Knit into the **front** of the second st on the left needle, then **purl** the first st, letting both sts drop off the needle at the same time.

BODY (Make 2)
Cast on 51 sts.

Row 1: K2, P2, (K3, P2) across to last 2 sts, K2.

Row 2 (Right side)**:** K4, P3, (K2, P3) across to last 4 sts, K4.

Row 3: K2, P2, (K3, P2) across to last 2 sts, K2.

Row 4: K2, CR, (P3, CR) across to last 2 sts, K2.

Rows 5-11: Repeat Rows 1-4 once, then repeat Rows 1-3 once **more**.

Row 12: K2, CR, (P3, CR) twice, P 23, CR, (P3, CR) twice, K2.

Row 13: K2, P2, (K3, P2) twice, K 23, P2, (K3, P2) twice, K2.

Row 14: K4, (P3, K2) twice, P 23, (K2, P3) twice, K4.

Row 15: K2, P2, (K3, P2) twice, K8, P1, K 14, P2, (K3, P2) twice, K2.

Row 16: K2, CR, (P3, CR) twice, P 14, K1, P8, CR, (P3, CR) twice, K2.

Row 17: K2, P2, (K3, P2) twice, K8, P1, K5, P1, K8, P2, (K3, P2) twice, K2.

Row 18: K4, (P3, K2) twice, P8, K1, P5, K1, P8, (K2, P3) twice, K4.

Row 19: K2, P2, (K3, P2) twice, K8, P1, K5, P1, K8, P2, (K3, P2) twice, K2.

Row 20: K2, CR, (P3, CR) twice, P8, TL, P3, TR, P8, CR, (P3, CR) twice, K2.

Row 21: K2, P2, (K3, P2) twice, K9, P1, K3, P1, K9, P2, (K3, P2) twice, K2.

Row 22: K4, (P3, K2) twice, P9, TL, P1, TR, P9, (K2, P3) twice, K4.

Row 23: K2, P2, (K3, P2) twice, K 10, P1, K1, P1, K 10, P2, (K3, P2) twice, K2.

Row 24: K2, CR, (P3, CR) twice, P 10, slip next 2 sts onto cable needle and hold in **back** of work, K1 from left needle, (P1, K1) from cable needle, P 10, CR, (P3, CR) twice, K2.

Row 25: K2, P2, (K3, P2) twice, K 10, P1, K1, P1, K 10, P2, (K3, P2) twice, K2.

Row 26: K4, (P3, K2) twice, P9, TR, P1, TL, P9, (K2, P3) twice, K4.

Row 27: K2, P2, (K3, P2) twice, K9, P1, K3, P1, K9, P2, (K3, P2) twice, K2.

Row 28: K2, CR, (P3, CR) twice, P8, TR, P3, TL, P8, CR, (P3, CR) twice, K2.

Row 29: K2, P2, (K3, P2) twice, K8, P1, K5, P1, K8, P2, (K3, P2) twice, K2.

Row 30: K4, (P3, K2) twice, P8, K1, P5, K1, P8, (K2, P3) twice, K4.

Row 31: K2, P2, (K3, P2) twice, K8, P1, K5, P1, K8, P2, (K3, P2) twice, K2.

Row 32: K2, CR, (P3, CR) twice, P8, K1, P5, K1, P8, CR, (P3, CR) twice, K2.

Row 33: K2, P2, (K3, P2) twice, K8, P1, K5, P1, K8, P2, (K3, P2) twice, K2.

Row 34: K4, (P3, K2) twice, P8, TL, P3, TR, P8, (K2, P3) twice, K4.

Row 35: K2, P2, (K3, P2) twice, K9, M1, P1, K3 tog, P1, M1 K9, P2, (K3, P2) twice, K2.

Row 36: K2, CR, (P3, CR) twice, P 10, slip next 2 sts onto cable needle and hold in **back** of work, P1 from left needle, P2 from cable needle, P 10, CR, (P3, CR) twice, K2.

Row 37: K2, P2, (K3, P2) twice, K23, P2, (K3, P2) twice, K2.

Row 38: K4, (P3, K2) twice, P23, (K2, P3) twice, K4.

Row 39: K2, P2, (K3, P2) twice, K23, P2, (K3, P2) twice, K2.

Row 40: K2, CR, (P3, CR) twice, P23, CR, (P3, CR) twice, K2.

Row 41: K2, P2, (K3, P2) across to last 2 sts, K2.

Row 42: K4, P3, (K2, P3) across to last 4 sts, K4.

Row 43: K2, P2, (K3, P2) across to last 2 sts, K2.

Row 44: K2, CR, (P3, CR) across to last 2 sts, K2.

Row 45: K2, P2, (K1, K2 tog, P2) across to last 2 sts, K2: 42 sts.

Row 46: K4, P2, (K2, P2) across to last 4 sts, K4.

Row 47: K2, (P2, K2) across.

Row 48: K2, CR, (P2, CR) across to last 2 sts, K2.

Row 49: K2, P2, (K2 tog, P2) across to last 2 sts, K2: 33 sts.

Row 50: K4, P1, (K2, P1) across to last 4 sts, K4.

Row 51: K2, P2, (K1, P2) across to last 2 sts, K2.

Row 52: K2, K2 tog, (P1, K2 tog) across to last 2 sts, K2: 23 sts.

Row 53: K2, P1, (K1, P1) across to last 2 sts, K2.

Row 54 (Eyelet row)**:** K1, (K2 tog, YO) across to last 2 sts, K2.

Row 55: K3, P1, (K1, P1) across to last 3 sts, K3.

Row 56: K2, P1, (K1, P1) across to last 2 sts, K2.

Row 57: K3, P1, (K1, P1) across to last 3 sts, K3.

Bind off all sts in pattern, leaving a long end for sewing.

FINISHING

Thread yarn needle with long end. With **wrong** sides of Body pieces together and matching rows, sew end of rows together, leaving an opening for the handle on one side and an opening for the spout on opposite side.

Tie: Make an 18" (45.5 cm) twisted cord *(see Twisted Cord, page 93)*.

Weave Tie through YO's on Eyelet row and tie in a bow. ♥

General Instructions

ABBREVIATIONS

ch(s)	chain(s)
cm	centimeters
CR	Cross Right
K	knit
M1	Make One
M1P	Make One Purl
mm	millimeters
P	purl
P2SSO	pass 2 slipped stitches over
PSSO	pass slipped stitch over
Rnd(s)	Round(s)
RS	right side
SBK	slip-bead-knit
SSK	Slip, Slip, Knit
st(s)	stitch(es)
TL	Twist Left
tog	together
TR	Twist Right
WS	wrong side
YO	yarn over

★ — work instructions following ★ as many **more** times as indicated in addition to the first time.

† to † — work all instructions from first † to second † **as many** times as specified.

( ) or [ ] — work enclosed instructions **as many** times as specified by the number immediately following **or** contains explanatory remarks.

colon (:) — the number(s) given after a colon at the end of a row or round denote(s) the number of stitches you should have on that row or round.

Yarn Weight Symbol & Names	LACE 0	SUPER FINE 1	FINE 2	LIGHT 3	MEDIUM 4	BULKY 5	SUPER BULKY 6
Type of Yarns in Category	Fingering, size 10 crochet thread	Sock, Fingering, Baby	Sport, Baby	DK, Light Worsted	Worsted, Afghan, Aran	Chunky, Craft, Rug	Bulky, Roving
Knit Gauge Range* in Stockinette St to 4" (10 cm)	33-40** sts	27-32 sts	23-26 sts	21-24 sts	16-20 sts	12-15 sts	6-11 sts
Advised Needle Size Range	000-1	1 to 3	3 to 5	5 to 7	7 to 9	9 to 11	11 and larger

*GUIDELINES ONLY: The chart above reflects the most commonly used gauges and needle sizes for specific yarn categories.

** Lace weight yarns are usually knitted on larger needles to create lacy openwork patterns. Accordingly, a gauge range is difficult to determine. Always follow the gauge stated in your pattern.

GAUGE

Exact gauge is essential for proper size and fit. Before beginning your project, make a sample swatch in the yarn and needles specified in the individual instructions. After completing the swatch, measure it, counting your stitches and rows carefully. If your swatch is larger or smaller than specified, **make another, changing needle size to get the correct gauge**. Keep trying until you find the size needles that will give you the specified gauge.

KNIT TERMINOLOGY	
UNITED STATES	**INTERNATIONAL**
gauge =	tension
bind off =	cast off
yarn over (YO) =	yarn forward (yfwd) **or** yarn around needle (yrn)

MARKERS

As a convenience to you, we have used markers to help distinguish the beginning of a pattern or round. Place markers as instructed. You may use purchased markers or tie a length of contrasting color yarn around the needle. When you reach a marker on each row (round), slip it from the left needle to the right needle; remove it when no longer needed.

A split-ring marker is placed around the first stitch on the round to indicated the beginning of the round. Move it up at the end of each round.

▆▢▢▢ BEGINNER	Projects for first-time knitters using basic knit and purl stitches. Minimal shaping.	
▆▆▢▢ EASY	Projects using basic stitches, repetitive stitch patterns, simple color changes, and simple shaping and finishing.	
▆▆▆▢ INTERMEDIATE	Projects with a variety of stitches, such as basic cables and lace, simple intarsia, double-pointed needles and knitting in the round needle techniques, mid-level shaping and finishing.	
▆▆▆▆ EXPERIENCED	Projects using advanced techniques and stitches, such as short rows, fair isle, more intricate intarsia, cables, lace patterns, and numerous color changes.	

KNITTING NEEDLES																		
U.S.	0	1	2	3	4	5	6	7	8	9	10	10½	11	13	15	17	19	35	50
U.K.	13	12	11	10	9	8	7	6	5	4	3	2	1	00	000	---	---	---	---
Metric - mm	2	2.25	2.75	3.25	3.5	3.75	4	4.5	5	5.5	6	6.5	8	9	10	12.75	15	19	25

ZEROS

To consolidate the length of an involved pattern, Zeros are sometimes used so that all sizes can be combined. For example, decrease 4{1-0} st(s) evenly spaced across means the first size would decrease 4 sts, the second size would decrease one st, and the third size would do nothing.

DOUBLE-POINTED NEEDLES

The stitches are divided evenly between three or four double-pointed needles as specified in the individual pattern (*Fig. 1a*). Form a triangle or a square with the needles (*Figs. 1b & c*).

Do **not** twist the cast on ridge. With the working yarn coming from the stitch on the last needle and using the remaining needle, work across the stitches on the first needle.

You will now have an empty needle with which to work the stitches from the next needle. Work the first stitch of each needle firmly to prevent gaps. Continue working around without turning the work.

Fig. 1a

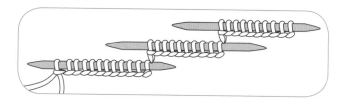

Fig. 1b

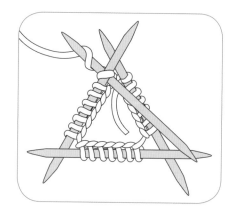

Fig. 1c

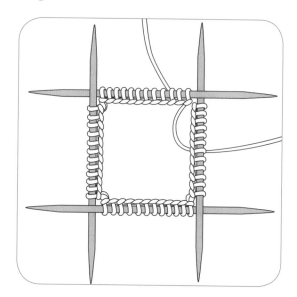

BACKWARD LOOP CAST ON

Make a backward loop with the working yarn and place it on the needle *(Fig. 2)*.

Fig. 2

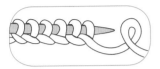

ADDING NEW STITCHES

Insert the right needle into the stitch as if to **knit**, yarn over and pull the loop through *(Fig. 3a)*, insert the left needle into the loop just worked from **front** to **back** and slip the loop onto the left needle *(Fig. 3b)*. Repeat for the required number of stitches.

Fig. 3a

Fig. 3b

YARN OVER

A yarn over *(abbreviated YO)* is simply placing the yarn over the right needle creating an extra stitch. Since the yarn over produces a hole in the knit fabric, it is used for a lacy effect. On the row following a yarn over, you must be careful to keep it on the needle and treat it as a stitch by knitting or purling it as instructed.

To make a yarn over, you'll loop the yarn over the needle like you would to knit or purl a stitch, bringing it either to the front or to the back of the piece so that it'll be ready to work the next stitch, creating a new stitch on the needle as follows:

After a knit stitch, before a knit stitch
Bring the yarn forward **between** the needles, then back **over** the top of the right hand needle, so that it is now in position to knit the next stitch *(Fig. 4a)*.

Fig. 4a

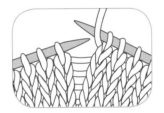

After a purl stitch, before a purl stitch
Take the yarn **over** the right hand needle to the back, then forward **under** it, so that it is now in position to purl the next stitch *(Fig. 4b)*.

Fig. 4b

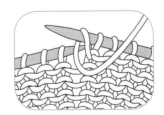

After a knit stitch, before a purl stitch

Bring the yarn forward **between** the needles, then back **over** the top of the right hand needle and forward **between** the needles again, so that it is now in position to purl the next stitch *(Fig. 4c)*.

Fig. 4c

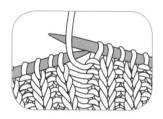

After a purl stitch, before a knit stitch

Take the yarn **over** the right hand needle to the back, so that it is now in position to knit the next stitch *(Fig. 4d)*.

Fig. 4d

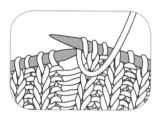

INCREASES
MAKE ONE *(abbreviated M1)*

Insert the left needle under the horizontal strand between the stitches from the **front** *(Fig. 5a)*. Then knit into the **back** of the strand *(Fig. 5b)*.

Fig. 5a

Fig. 5b

MAKE ONE PURL *(abbreviated M1P)*

Insert the left needle under the horizontal strand between the stitches from the **front** *(Fig. 6)*. Then purl into the **back** of the strand.

Fig. 6

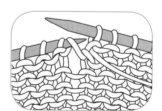

DECREASES

KNIT 2 TOGETHER (abbreviated K2 tog)

Insert the right needle into the **front** of the first two stitches on the left needle as if to knit **(Fig. 7)**, then **knit** them together as if they were one stitch.

Fig. 7

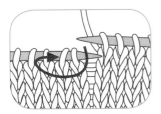

PURL 2 TOGETHER (abbreviated P2 tog)

Insert the right needle into the **front** of the first two stitches on the left needle as if to **purl (Fig. 8)**, then **purl** them together as if they were one stitch.

Fig. 8

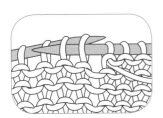

SLIP, SLIP, KNIT (abbreviated SSK)

With yarn held in back of work, separately slip two stitches as if to **knit (Fig. 9a)**. Insert the **left** needle into the **front** of both slipped stitches **(Fig. 9b)** and **knit** them together as if they were one stitch **(Fig. 9c)**.

Fig. 9a

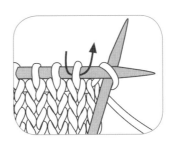

Fig. 9b

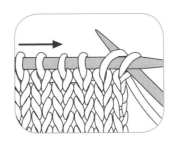

Fig. 9c

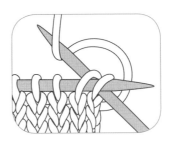

KNIT 3 TOGETHER (abbreviated K3 tog)

Insert the right needle into the **front** of the first three stitches on the left needle as if to **knit** *(Fig. 10)*, then **knit** them together as if they were one stitch.

Fig. 10

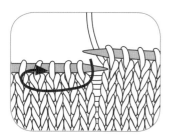

PURL 3 TOGETHER (abbreviated P3 tog)

Insert the right needle into the **front** of the first three stitches on the left needle as if to **purl** *(Fig. 11)*, then **purl** them together as if they were one stitch.

Fig. 11

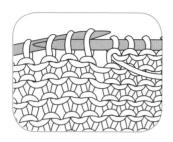

SLIP 1, KNIT 2 TOGETHER, PASS SLIPPED STITCH OVER
(abbreviated slip 1, K2 tog, PSSO)

Slip one stitch as if to **knit** *(Fig. 12a)*, then knit the next two stitches together *(Fig. 7, page 91)*. With the left needle, bring the slipped stitch over the stitch just made *(Fig. 12b)* and off the needle.

Fig. 12a

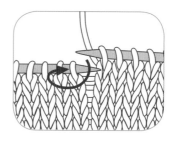

Fig. 12b

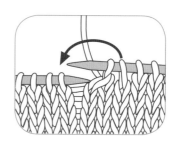

SLIP 2 TOGETHER, KNIT 1, PASS 2 SLIPPED STITCHES OVER

(abbreviated slip 2 tog, K1, P2SSO)

With yarn in back, slip two stitches together as if to **knit** *(Fig. 13a)*, then knit the next stitch. With the left needle, bring both slipped stitches over the knit stitch *(Fig. 13b)* and off the needle.

Fig. 13a

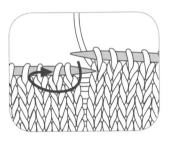

Fig. 13b

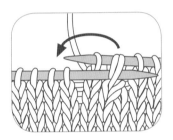

TWISTED CORD

Cut 2 pieces of yarn, each **3 times** as long as the desired finished length. Holding both pieces together, fasten one end to a stationary object **or** have another person hold it; twist until **tight**. Fold in half and let it twist itself, knot both ends and cut the loops on the folded end.

PICKING UP STITCHES

When instructed to pick up stitches from the **right** side, insert the needle from the **front** to the **back** under two strands at the edge of the worked piece. Put the yarn around the needle as if to **knit** *(Fig. 14a or b)*, then bring the needle with the yarn back through the stitch to the right side, resulting in a stitch on the needle. When instructed to pick up stitches from the **wrong** side, insert the needle from the **back** to the **front**. Put the yarn around the needle as if to **purl** *(Fig. 14c)*, then bring the needle with the yarn back through the stitch to the wrong side, resulting in a stitch on the needle. Repeat this along the edge, picking up the required number of stitches.

A crochet hook may be helpful to pull yarn through.

Fig. 14a

Fig. 14b

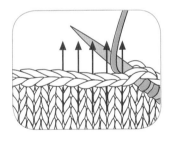

Fig. 14c

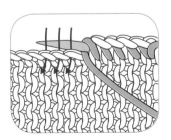

Yarn Information

TRAVELING SHAWL
Jojoland™ Melody Superwash
#MS06

ENTRELAC SHAWL
Version 1 - Knit Picks® Palette™
Lt Pink - #23718 Blush
Med Pink - #24570 Blossom Heather
Dk Pink - #24569 Cotton Candy
Version 2 - Jojoland™ Melody Superwash
MS47

HEADBAND & FINGERLESS GLOVES
Plymouth Select Plymouth Yarn®
Worsted Merino Superwash
#21

CRESCENT SHAWL
Jojoland™ Melody Superwash
#MS06

BEADED TRAVELING SHAWL
Rowan Kidsilk Haze
#580 Grace

TRAVELING SCARF
Jojoland™ Melody Superwash
#MS14

STOCKING CAP
Berroco® Vintage™
#5123 Blush

SCARF
Berroco® Vintage™
#5123 Blush

The projects in this book were made using a variety of yarns and threads. Any brand in the specified weight may be used. It is best to refer to the yardage/meters when determining how many balls or skeins to purchase. Remember, to arrive at the finished size, it is the GAUGE/TENSION that is important, not the brand of yarn. For your convenience, listed below are the specific yarns and threads used to create our photography models.

FACE CLOTH
Ella Rae Milky Soft
#91220

BOOKMARK
Aunt Lydia's® Fashion Crochet Cotton Thread, Size 3
#0775 Warm Rose

CARD INSERT
Aunt Lydia's® Fashion Crochet Cotton Thread, Size 3
#0775 Warm Rose
We used Strathmore Photo Frame Cards
www.strathmoreartist.com

ENTRELAC PILLOW
Premier Yarns™ Deborah Norville Collection Everyday™ Soft Worsted
ED100-06 Baby Pink

HOT WATER BOTTLE COVER
Knit Picks® Comfy Bulky™
#B982 Flamingo

LAP THROW
Lion Brand® Cotton Ease®
#112 Berry

MUG COZY
Knit Picks® Comfy Worsted™
#5606 Peony

SACHET OR SOAP COVER
Ella Rae Milky Soft
#91220

TEAPOT COZY
Knit Picks® Comfy Worsted™
#5606 Peony

Project Journal

DATE	RECIPIENT	PATTERN NAME	YARN USED	YARDAGE	NEEDLE SIZE

To: _____

From: _____

Date: _____

CARE INSTRUCTIONS

_____
_____
_____
_____

Leisure Arts, Inc. grants permission to the owner of this book to copy this page for personal use only.